Peconic Bay Publishing
Southampton, NY 11968

© George M. Motz, 2019

The author has tried to recreate events, locations, and conversations from interviews and the collected stories and memories of all referenced herein. The author has made every effort to give credit to the source of any images, quotes, or other material contained herein and obtain permissions when feasible.

ISBN: 9781090434289

Printed in the United States of America

FOREWORD

The Vietnam Era draws many different emotions from those who were of 'Military Age' in the 1960s and 1970s. Some fought. Some fled. All of us of that generation were affected in some way.

Newspaper headlines showed the youth of America demonstrating in the streets placed alongside blaring headlines of other young men and women killed in the then remote country of Vietnam. "Why," they cried, "Must so many die?" Clearly, the war was unpopular with those who served in the hot, steamy jungles as well as with those who demonstrated at home. Yet most missed the greatest tragedy of all -- the everlasting impact of lives lost on the families of those men and women.

Lieutenant George Motz served his years of active duty in the continental United States with the responsibility of dealing personally with those grieving families who had lost a child, a parent, or other close relative, a beloved family member who would never again be around to celebrate Christmas or the Fourth of July with them.

FOREWORD

I volunteered to serve in one of America's most selective units, the U.S. Navy SEALS. Very difficult training for some of our most dangerous missions. Lieutenant Motz volunteered as well and received an assignment far removed from his geographic roots, expectations, or training. Two young men from Long Island, swimming together on the summer days of their youth, now thrust into challenging assignments.

I had the easier task. We had visible, physical tools to use in the conduct of our missions. Lt. Motz had none, other than his instinct during his daily encounters with shattered families. Standing on one front porch after another, in Deep South neighborhoods unfamiliar to him, preparing to destroy the dreams of a family. Picture the movie 'Groundhog Day' but without the humor. What can you possibly do to best help those families in their time of need? What he found through experience was an unexpected sense of humanity, an ability to relate to those families, all of whom he discovered had an inherent strength which enabled them to deal with their grief. Families from all levels of society, most frequently poor black families facing simultaneously the impact of an unpopular war plus racial unrest at home, yet able, through perseverance and a strong religious spirit, to gradually put their lives somewhat back in order.

These families did not seek headlines. They sought the answer to "Why?" Every day was another family that needed his help and every day Lt. Motz responded. I don't know how he dealt with this amazing burden, but I thank him for bringing this 'Hidden Toll', not just of the Vietnam War but of all wars, to our attention.

Thomas R. Richards
Rear Admiral, U.S. Navy, (Ret.)

INTRODUCTION

It seems so long ago! Over fifty years and counting since I was assigned to work with families who had suffered the unthinkable loss of a loved one in a war embraced by no one. Loved ones cut down in the prime of their life. Fifty years ago, and yet my memories of that assignment remain crystal clear to this day. So much pain inflicted by my in-person death notices and so little I could say or do to relieve that pain.

Traditionally, great honor is bestowed upon military personnel who have given their life to protect and defend our country. Nothing could be more fitting or proper. But what about a parent who has lost a son or daughter, a husband or wife who has lost a life partner, or a soldier's children, who will grow up without a mom or dad to guide them? Yes, they are comforted by family and friends in the days and weeks following the untimely death, but what about the never-ending sense of loss? They say that time heals all wounds, but for those families, the wounds they are forced to live with never fully heal.

This story focuses on my personal experiences with families suffering the loss of a loved one during the Vietnam War, starting in the winter of 1964-65. I began that year brimming with confidence and looking forward to a new chapter in my life as I made the big leap from the insulated life of academia into the real world. That high level of confidence would prove to be, at the very least, woefully premature. At first, everything was about as expected; a rigorous boot camp for young officers in Virginia, followed by a stateside posting to an Army depot in Charleston, South Carolina. That predictable pattern was broken, however, on the day I reported for duty and was appointed the area Survivors Assistance officer, a position for which I had absolutely no formal military or civilian training. It would prove to be an assignment that would test

2

my mettle and force me to become a full-fledged grownup overnight. More importantly, once mastered, it would have an all-encompassing impact on my post-military life, heavily influencing my career choices, my parenting style, and my overall philosophy on interpersonal relationships.

Coincidently, my first year of active duty exactly paralleled the massive build-up of American forces in Vietnam, troops assigned there to fight in a war that many respected historians have long judged to be the most unpopular war in our country's history. The reasons for that are widely known and arguably justified. Nevertheless, the fact remains that over 58,000 good and honorable American men and women lost their lives simply for answering the call to serve their country. Add to that total the hundreds of thousands of mothers, fathers, husbands, wives, children, brothers, sisters, and other close relatives affected by those deaths, the silent sufferers, and the picture takes on an even darker and more tragic tone.

This story explores the gut-wrenching impact of the Vietnam War on families from every conceivable social and economic background, with a somewhat special focus on the Southern black family. Clearly, the loss of a loved one was devastating to all families, but for the black family, the loss was compounded by the racially-charged environment of the mid-1960s. Although most of those black families lived in the larger cities of southeastern South Carolina, several lived in extremely isolated Gullah/Geechee communities, a century or more removed from the modern world. Working with those families gave me a rare, uncensored look into the lives of people who, at least from a materialistic perspective, were less fortunate than myself: decent, hardworking folks surviving on the edge of poverty with minimal opportunities for advancement, and then forced upon my visit, to deal with an unthinkable tragedy. It also gave me, a transplanted New Yorker, a rare opportunity to bear witness to the surprising

INTRODUCTION

treatment of black families in mourning by their Southern white neighbors and local law enforcement personnel. Yes, I had been told what to expect, yet the reality was quite different.

I lived with all of those grief-stricken families, day-in and day-out, for over two years and witnessed first-hand the grace, fortitude, and amazing strength of character they exhibited throughout their ordeal. Good people to the core. This is their story.

George M. Motz
Quogue, New York
2019

TABLE OF CONTENTS

PREFACE

"After you make your death notification to that soldier's family in Monck's Corner, I'd like you to go to a Ku Klux Klan rally tonight up there in Summerville to get a sense of how hostile they are to colored folks in these parts." The speaker: my Commanding Officer, Colonel C.S. Campbell. The time: the early spring of 1966. The place: Charleston, South Carolina. My experience in delivering an in-person death notice: *minimal.* It was a new Army initiative. My experience in race relations: *minimal.* I grew up in an all-white suburb of New York City. My options to pass on an evening with the KKK: *none.* It was a direct order.

And that was just one of dozens of unique experiences and opportunities afforded me during my posting to the Charleston Army Depot, all of which helped to shape my life beyond the military. Some of the experiences were one-of-a-kind: the KKK rally, court ordered best man at a quickie wedding, and judge at a Miss America beauty pageant, as were some of the opportunities: a highly prized chance to briefly meet with Dr. Martin Luther King, Jr., at the South Carolina Southern Christian Leadership Conference Penn Center headquarters in Frogmore. Others were ongoing but not particularly time-consuming. For example, as the Army representative on the Greater Charleston Armed Forces Disciplinary Control Board, I was responsible for periodic evaluations of a legendary house of prostitution plus dozens of others, all vying to cater to the heavy military presence in the area. That said, the vast amount of my time and effort focused on one assignment only: working with families mourning the war-related loss of a loved one, from initial notification through memorial services and beyond.

This is a story I have always wanted to tell. Why? Simply because it speaks of a time in our country more than fifty years ago dominated by two very powerful and difficult challenges: the increasingly unpopular war in Vietnam and the fight at home for racial equality. Of course, millions of Americans lived through that period; however, few were positioned, as was I, to witness on a daily basis, the harsh impact of those two major issues on the lives of individuals most directly affected by them.

Fair enough, but what finally motivated me to write about it now, a half-century later? The answer: my shock at the senseless killing of nine innocent blacks in June of 2015 at Mother Emanuel AME Church in Charleston, including one lady with whom I had worked on several memorial services long ago. A truly wonderful woman who provided both desperately needed help to families facing a terrible loss and sage advice to me concerning specific customs related to black memorial services. Her murder was so tragic and, in a very real way, so personal to me. It was time to tell my story.

But how to tell the story? One could easily argue that it should be told in strict chronological order, the simplest way to convey the reality of the times: month after month of increasing casualties. Although that made perfect sense on one level, it seemed to completely ignore the human side of the story. A better approach, I determined, was one which gave me the flexibility to flesh out and analyze the impact of several common scenarios faced by those families during the most difficult period of their lives.

Finally, a word of thanks is in order to those who worked alongside me in fulfilling my assignment, especially the ministers and funeral home directors, all of whom worked tirelessly to help those suffering from the loss of a loved one. A salute also to the Honor Guard units from Ft. Jackson and Ft. McPherson who always made the final tribute to the soldiers so very special for the families in their time of grief. And, in a broader sense, my sincerest praise to all the people of South Carolina, black and white alike, who unfailingly showed genuine sympathy and respect to the families of all the soldiers killed in the war, regardless of the color of the soldier's skin. Quite remarkable considering the times. Last but not least, my deepest appreciation to my Commanding Officer, Colonel C.S. Campbell, who taught me many valuable lessons about dealing successfully with life's challenges.

CHAPTER 1

My Introduction to the Military Life.

The scene is forever etched in my soul. In the background, the peaceful, yet haunting sound of a bugler blowing Taps for another young soldier killed in action in Vietnam. In the foreground, a large group of family and friends gathered together at graveside under a hot and humid South Carolina sun grieving over a loved one lost for a cause few of them understood. This assignment, early in my adult life, would prove to be a unique and invaluable experience for me, one that I certainly never sought or expected, but unquestionably one which would come to define my goals and objectives in life.

By any measure, my childhood was idyllic. I grew up in an upper middle-class suburb of New York City with my parents and two sisters, Virginia, older by several years and my twin sister, Susan. My father, who passed away shortly after my eighth birthday, was a successful businessman and championship-caliber golfer with an extraordinarily outgoing personality who numbered several larger-than-life individuals, including Babe Ruth, among his many good friends. I attended a Catholic grammar school in my village and upon graduation, went to and graduated from the local public high school. For college, I chose a liberal arts program at Georgetown University in Washington, D.C. with a concentration in History and Philosophy. I also joined the Army R.O.T.C. program on the advice of my mother who correctly sensed that the troubles in Vietnam were going to get much worse and it therefore made sense to earn my commission and enter the military as an officer. Wise advice in hindsight. It was also the Kennedy years in the White House, a wonderful time to be a student in our nation's capital. Four happy years later, on the morning of June the 10th of 1963 I was

10

commissioned a second lieutenant in the United States Army and then awarded a Bachelor of Arts degree in History and Philosophy during the University convocation later that afternoon. A very good day indeed and certainly a very positive start to my adult life.

Following graduation from Georgetown, I took what seemed a logical next step: applying for and receiving an academic deferment to attend law school at Fordham University School of Law in New York. After completing my first year at Fordham, I chose to opt out of my student deferment and begin my two-year active duty commitment; reasoning that, with Vietnam heating up by the day, it made sense to put my active duty obligation behind me and then continue my pursuit of a law degree. The Army was happy to bring me on board and I was ordered to report to the Quartermaster School at Ft. Lee in Petersburg, Virginia, about 30 miles south of Richmond, in late December of 1964.

Much had changed during the 18-month period between my college graduation and yearend 1964, on both the domestic and international fronts. At home, racial tensions, building over many decades, had reached the boiling point. The "March for Civil Rights" in Birmingham, Alabama on May 2nd of 1963 led to a desegregation accord which, in turn, led to rioting. An attempt the following month by Governor George Wallace to keep the University of Alabama segregated failed but only when President Kennedy dispatched federal troops to the campus on June 11th to ensure compliance with federal law. Medgar Evers, a civil rights leader focused on black voter registration, was assassinated in front of his home in Jackson, Mississippi the following day. After a brief respite, thanks in large part to Dr. Martin Luther King, Jr.'s peaceful "March to Washington" and his iconic "I Have a Dream" speech at the Lincoln Memorial on August 28th, tensions once again took center stage, with the death of four young black girls during the bombing of Birmingham's 16th Street Baptist Church on September 15th. Conditions continued to deteriorate in 1964 with the murders of three civil rights workers in Mississippi in June, and unrest over the OMNIBUS Civil Rights legislation signed into law by President Lyndon B. Johnson in early August.

On the international front, our government was faced with difficult decisions concerning our support of the South Vietnamese government which was systematically being overrun by the Communist North. Yes, our commitment there was still technically an advisory one; however, in reality, that commitment was rapidly expanding, month by month, leaving most experts to conclude that we would soon end up in a long and costly war in support of the South Vietnamese.

With all of that in mind, I headed off to Ft. Lee, bags packed into my early edition 1965 Mustang convertible, dubbed a 1964 1/2 model by the press, frankly having absolutely no idea what to expect once I arrived. What I should have expected was boot camp for young officers. We were housed in a couple of old barracks, probably dating back to World War I, and treated like the raw recruits that, in hindsight, we were. The program combined classroom work with field study and it was quite rigorous.

The goal was twofold: to mold a class of approximately 60 new second lieutenants into leaders and, on a more basic level, to teach us the proper techniques for setting up, operating, and dismantling the tools of the quartermaster trade under battlefield conditions. One thing I quickly learned: as an Army officer, you would be given challenging assignments early in your career, and you would be fully expected to carry out those assignments, on schedule, exactly as directed. Failure was not an option.

A typical day at Ft. Lee began with reveille just

before sunrise and concluded with Taps at 2200 hours. Each week brought its own set of challenges: one week learning how to operate equipment typically used by the quartermaster, the fork-lift truck for example, another week learning how to fire and range qualify on the M-14 rifle, the newest rifle available for the troops. That training was continuously combined with quartermaster field exercises each lasting a couple of days, and an ongoing physical fitness program.

On the leadership side, and in keeping with the primary mission of training us as officers, we were subjected to rotating assignments on a daily basis with next day roles posted on the barrack's bulletin board at 1900 hours each evening. As a result, you could easily find yourself one day as a squad member and then a platoon leader or even company commander the next, making for an interesting leadership challenge.

Toward the end of the eighth week of the program, we were given our permanent assignments. Somewhat fatalistic by nature, I fully expected to hear Vietnam when my name was called out at reveille but instead I heard Charleston, South Carolina. What a shock! Not that I knew anything about Charleston, but it sounded like a plum assignment, a feeling confirmed by two of my classmates, graduates of The Citadel in Charleston, who quickly offered to switch assignments with me. The final tally: a half dozen classmates were assigned directly to Vietnam, another half dozen to Germany, and the balance to various stateside posts scattered around the country. I later discovered that almost three quarters of the class, myself included, did eventually receive orders to Vietnam during our initial tour of duty.

The graduation ceremony on the morning of March the 5th was presided over by the Post Commandant, Major General Hugh MacIntosh, and it was basically a 45-minute pep talk followed by the distribution of our diplomas. With my bags packed beforehand, I was on the road heading south down I-95 less than an hour after dismissal, arriving in the Charleston area at dusk. Although I could have spent the night at the Charleston Air Force Base BOQ (Bachelor Officer Quarters), I opted to find an inexpensive motel near the Depot in North Charleston. My first sensation as I stepped out of my car was the temperature: 70 degrees on an early March evening, not at all what I had grown accustomed to in the Northeast. The second sensation occurred at check-in: hearing the deep Southern drawl for the first time. It was so pronounced that I couldn't help but wonder if perhaps it was part of a public relations effort put on for visitors from up North. Certainly, that girl didn't talk like that on a normal day-to-day basis, or did she? Before the first week was over I realized the accents were absolutely authentic.

Following a decent night's sleep, I showered, dressed in my Army greens, drove to a nearby diner on the Dual Lane Highway, and devoured a breakfast of bacon, fried eggs over easy, and my first bowl of grits topped with plenty of fresh creamy butter. I then covered the final two miles up Remount Road to the Charleston Army Depot which I couldn't help but notice was located right next door to a huge and very active pulp and paper mill which was billowing white clouds of sweet-smelling smoke into the air and, frankly, awfully close to the ground. That aroma has stayed with me to this day.

The Depot was fenced off and guarded at the main gate by civilian guards, not by a Military Police detail as I would have expected. Once I had identified myself to the guard on duty, I was directed to the Headquarters Building which he indicated was outside the main gate and just beyond a railroad storage yard. "Hard to miss it" he cheerfully assured me. Once there, I asked for Colonel Campbell, whom I knew was expecting me and, in a matter of minutes, I was ushered into his office by his secretary,

Marguerite Rickenbaker.

The colonel, a tall gentleman looking to be in his early fifties, greeted me warmly, asked me to take a seat, and proceeded to give me a thorough overview of the Depot's mission. I first learned that the facility was spread out over several hundred acres with substantial frontage on the Cooper River. I was then told that the facility was staffed by over 300 employees, almost all of whom were civilians. The military presence was indeed small, only seven officers and two enlisted men, a medic and a staff sergeant specializing in transportation repair and storage.

"The primary mission of the Depot" the colonel noted, "is the repair and storage of the Army's large fleet of tug boats and harbor craft in the 60-110 foot range, and Army landing craft...LCMs and LCUs dating back to World War II and the Korean conflict."

"Also on site," he continued, "are a number of amphibious vehicles, similar in size to the LCMs plus a few huge LARC-5s."

"In addition," he concluded, "the Depot's mission also includes repair and storage of the Army's rather large rail fleet including several diesel locomotives, and hundreds of box cars, flat cars, tank cars, and passenger cars, all supported by a fully operational roundhouse."

All in all, fun stuff for someone who grew up around boats and model trains.

From a chain of command perspective, the colonel indicated that I would be reporting directly to the captain in charge of the Administration & Services Division, and that I would be working directly with Mrs. Doris Bercaw, whom he assured me was one of the most respected employees at the Depot. Finally, he mentioned that as a single officer, I would need to find my own off-Post housing which he was certain would not be a problem because of the very positive attitude towards the military throughout the Charleston community.

CHAPTER 1

At the end of the briefing, Colonel Campbell officially appointed me the new Military Personnel Officer, an Adjutant General position in Army lingo, not the Quartermaster slot that I had trained for and expected. Yet another lesson about the Army: as an officer, you were expected to be flexible and, if necessary, learn on the job.

It didn't take long for me to grasp the scope of my new assignment. In the broadest sense, I needed to become generally familiar with all existing Army rules and regulations pertaining to personnel matters, with a particular focus on new and/or revised ones and to make that information available to interested Army personnel either assigned to the Depot or living in the Greater Charleston area. Of course, there were only a handful of active duty Army personnel assigned to the Depot and they all tended to be well-versed on existing regulations.

There were, however, a large number of retired Army personnel and their families living in the greater Charleston area. Although that seemed a bit odd to me at first since the nearest large Army facility, Ft. Jackson, was a full two hour drive up I-26, I quickly discovered that Charleston was an ideal retirement community for all military personnel regardless of their branch of service. Why? Simply because it offered a pleasant year-round climate in a spectacular antebellum setting and a full-service hospital at the Naval Base as well as several other world class medical facilities in the downtown area. It also offered a great choice of quality restaurants, extensive cultural options such as the Dock Street Theater, and two very large and fully stocked PX and Commissary facilities, one each at the Naval and Air Force Bases. The most common assistance that our office offered to the retirees was responding to frequent requests for clarification of new rules and regulations and authorizing and issuing new or replacement military ID cards.

My assignment came with a number of other

responsibilities, most of which were part time in nature. As the Special Services Officer, for example, I was responsible for operating the Depot swimming pool, something I was quite familiar with thanks to many years lifeguarding during summers in the Hamptons. The only challenge with the pool was keeping the water chemically safe for swimming thanks to the clouds of toxic smoke from our neighbor. As part of that duty, I also held the purse strings to the Unit Fund which reserved small amounts of money for the Depot officers to spend quarterly, usually on a day of deep-sea fishing in the Gulf Stream.

Barely noticeable among my 16 or 17 assignments were two that would completely overwhelm the others and become the basis for this story: Casualty Notification and Survivors Assistance. To be sure, the Survivors Assistance function in peacetime was pretty much limited to helping the next of kin of retired Army personnel resolve outstanding estate issues of a military nature, usually weeks if not months, after the retiree's death. In wartime, however, that function took on a powerful life of its own. Work on a Survivors Assistance case involving an active duty soldier killed in action began within hours of the reported death and it was substantially more stressful. As challenging as that responsibility was, the front half of that assignment, the actual in-person notification, was immeasurably more difficult. Never did I have a case where the next-of-kin's family was prepared to hear the devastating news that I had for them. Their reactions ranged from tearful acceptance to denial, and increasingly over time, to anger directed at the Army for allowing the unthinkable to happen in a war they often found difficult to embrace.

CHAPTER 2

Survivors Assistance - Retired Personnel:
Easing into my new assignment.

My learning curve in Survivors Assistance evolved chronologically through three well-defined timeframes: first working with the next-of-kin of retired Army personnel, then working with families in receipt of a Western Union battlefield death notice, and finally, personally delivering the tragic news to a family's doorstep. In hindsight, the three-step process proved to be a fortuitous one in that it afforded me the opportunity to learn and grow on the job, so that by the time I was involved in the complete process, I pretty much knew what to expect, and was therefore less likely to be blindsided along the way.

With that thought in mind, I'd like to take a brief look at that first step--Survivors Assistance--Retired Personnel--and then move quickly on to the more complex cases involving very young active duty soldiers killed in the line of duty.

My first Survivors Assistance case arrived at my desk at the start of my third week as the Military Personnel Officer. A woman called and asked for help in settling her late husband's military affairs. In the course of our conversation, she indicated that he had served as an officer in the Army for over 35 years and had retired to Charleston in the early-1950s with the rank of full colonel. She further indicated that he had passed away peacefully in his sleep several weeks earlier following a short illness. After sharing some other background information with me, I suggested that we get together, either at my office or at her home, whichever was more convenient for her. She seemed genuinely pleased to accept my offer of a visit to her home but asked for a couple of days to organize her thoughts. Since I also needed some time to do the same, we agreed to schedule the visit for early the following week. Fortunately, thanks to our brief conversation, I knew the types of questions she would be asking, and I had a pretty good idea where to find the answers. A couple of days later, when I felt I had a decent handle on her case, I called and set up a visit to her home for the following Monday afternoon.

The drive from the Depot to her home just across the Ashley River Bridge from downtown Charleston on a beautiful early spring afternoon was quick and totally relaxing. Her home was located in a very nice and relatively new subdivision of well-maintained homes, manicured lawns, and beautiful gardens with spring flowers in full bloom. As soon as she saw me walking up her front path, she threw open the front door, welcomed me warmly, and ushered me straight into the dining room, which she was using as a temporary office for organizing her husband's estate.

After a few minutes of small talk focused on the joys of living in Charleston and how happy she was that they had chosen it for their retirement, she turned her focus to questions she needed answered, all quite naturally pertaining to her new status as a retired officer's widow. Questions on what, if any, benefits she might lose, with a particular emphasis on her health care benefits. She also had a number of financial questions relating to their various banking accounts and his military life insurance policy. What I found interesting was that just about every question she asked led her to reminisce at great length about life with her husband going back to his early days in the Army during the very late stages of World War I. Since I really hadn't spent any time focused on what a career in the military might be like, I found those stories not only interesting but also helpful in giving me a better appreciation of what to expect should I eventually decide to turn my initial obligation into a full-time career.

Following a couple hours of work, she suggested we take a break for afternoon tea on her outdoor patio where we continued our mutual praise of all things Charleston while munching on some freshly-baked chocolate chip cookies. By the time I left her home an hour or so later, I had more than enough information to complete my Survivors Assistance work at the office. Only one step remained: her visit to my office the following week to pick up her new military ID card.

Overall, this initial experience was a positive one for me in all respects. I also came away from it with a far better understanding of the Survivors Assistance role. Not only was I expected to resolve the next of kin's military issues, I was also given the opportunity to participate, albeit in a very small way, in their healing process.

Over the next six to nine months, several dozen additional Survivors Assistance cases surfaced, all involving retired military personnel. Apparently, word had gotten out very quickly within that close-knit community, that the Depot was available to help families deal with their issues, an attractive alternative to making the four-hour round-trip trek to Ft. Jackson up in Columbia. In general, the cases tended to follow a similar pattern: a telephone call to my office from the widow or occasionally her attorney or accountant, a personal visit to her home in the greater Charleston area, and a resolution of all military-related issues. Each case also led me to a greater understanding of the grieving process and my role in it. In addition, as I was soon to discover, the solid background I was building in Survivors Assistance would become an invaluable asset as I stepped up to the next level of my assignment.

And what a step it was! On a late March morning in 1966, I received my first official Casualty Notification assignment involving an active duty soldier killed in the line of duty in Vietnam.

CHAPTER 3

Casualty Notification Plus Survivors Assistance:
The heartbreak of delivering in-person death notifications.

By the end of 1965, it had become patently obvious to just about everyone that the war in Vietnam wasn't going to end anytime soon. Somewhat ironically, at least from my personal perspective, the first combat troops had landed on Vietnamese soil on March the 8th of that year, the same day I was appointed Survivors Assistance Officer at the Depot. In hindsight, it was an omen of things to come. The 3,500-man unit, 3rd Marine Regiment, 3rd Marine Battalion, that came ashore in Da Nang Province, was the start of an American build-up that hit 185,000 just nine months later, finally peaking at 543,000 in April of 1969. The press had a very active presence in the war zone and did a thorough job reporting the rising casualty numbers as more and more of our troops were placed in harm's way.

During the early stages of the Vietnam War, individual casualty notifications were made "the old-fashioned way" – delivered to the next-of-kin by a Western Union messenger. That protocol was eliminated and officially replaced Army-wide on March 15, 1966 by an in-person notification program using the services of a field grade officer (major or above) on a rotating basis. The goal was to create "a more personalized procedure using the military to initiate the process," after which he or she would notify headquarters to authorize the release of the official telegram to the next-of-kin and family. This was a very important initiative, especially as tolerance toward the war effort waned.

Our first exposure to the new protocol came via a call from the Presidio, the West Coast Army Headquarters in San Francisco, less than two weeks after its introduction. A young soldier had been shot and killed while on patrol just north of Saigon and his next-of-kin, his parents, lived just east of Charleston in a small black community on the outskirts of Mt. Pleasant. The colonel chose me to make the notification in spite of my junior grade. His logic: I was the Military Personnel Officer and already handling the back half of the assignment, Survivors Assistance, for both retired and active duty soldiers with positive feedback, so why not? Unspoken of course, the other more senior officers were legitimately very busy and the new assignment certainly wasn't going to be an enjoyable one for anyone.

The key was the timing. Under the new protocol, the notification had to be made same day, by 2100 hours. With that in mind, I placed a call to the Presidio to get basic timeline information relating to the return of the soldier, quickly memorized the brief official statement that I would deliver to the family, jumped into my car, and headed to Mt. Pleasant. Several miles into the trip, the magnitude of the assignment hit me full force and I pulled off to the side of the road for several minutes to gather my wits. My God, I was about to shatter a family's dreams, pure and simple. My mind raced trying to imagine how they would react to the news and how I would respond to their reaction. I simply had no answers to those very real questions and that was downright frightening.

Nevertheless, there was no turning back, so I continued on my way, pulling up in front of the soldier's home, where I parked my car, walked up the short path to the front porch, and knocked on the door. A pleasant looking black woman, probably in her mid-forties, answered my knock with a quizzical look on her face and, upon my request, identified herself as the soldier's mother. I then recited from memory the official notification speech:

"The President of the United States, the Department of the Army, and the People of the United States, regret to inform you that your son died as a result of a gunshot wound to the head. He died at approximately 1700 hours on March the 22nd in Da Nang Province, Vietnam."

Not surprisingly, she collapsed to the porch floor long before I had completed the second sentence. At that point, I had to rely purely on instinct, which told me to help her up, get her back into her home, seated someplace, on a couch or chair if one was nearby, and to keep talking to her in as calm and soothing a voice as I could muster. For some reason, I also raced into the kitchen and brought her a glass of water. Once she had gathered herself a bit, I started to explain the basics of what she could expect going forward: a daily visit from me during which time we would map out a plan for the upcoming memorial services, which I explained wouldn't take place for at least three weeks, the time it would take for her son to be returned from overseas. As I was explaining those steps to her, a neighbor seeing a car she did not recognize with New York State license plates parked out front, came rushing over, learned what had happened, and began to softly pray, which provided just the spark needed to help the mother cope with the terrible news that I had just delivered.

The following morning, I reported on my evening's work to Colonel Campbell and together we outlined my course of action for that case as well as for all others that he believed would most assuredly surface over the coming months due to the rapid buildup of troop strength in Vietnam and exacerbated locally by above average enlistment levels in South Carolina. The key going forward, he stressed, was to do whatever was necessary to demonstrate genuine compassion in each and every case so as to reflect well on the military in general and the Army in particular.

As promised, I visited with the family on a daily basis, a pattern I followed in all subsequent cases. Over time, we began to make plans for the wake and funeral services, which I was surprised to find became somewhat of a positive distraction for the family. On the 20th day, I received word from the Presidio that the body would arrive the following evening on a late night flight to the Charleston Air Force Base. With clearance obtained by Colonel Campbell, I was able to walk right onto the tarmac to observe the lowering of the casket from the cargo hold. I then followed the hearse to the funeral home in downtown Charleston. This also became my standard operating procedure, whether I was meeting a flight at the Air Force Base or Municipal Airport, or, on one or two occasions, a train at the Charleston train station.

For whatever reason, I assumed that I would simply check in with the funeral home that night and set a time to return the following day with the family. After all, it was now well past midnight. The funeral director, however, requested that I stay for a bit, asking me if I would be willing to inspect the body with him in order to determine the advisability of an open casket. Of course, that decision rested entirely with the family, but experience had shown him that in certain cases the remains were in such bad shape that a viewing by anyone other than a professional in the field had often proven to be very traumatic for those closest to the deceased. That should have been my warning. Nevertheless, since I didn't feel that I could refuse the request, I agreed to take a look. Absolutely nothing could have prepared me for what I saw. The back of the soldier's head had been largely blown away and the face was just barely recognizable from the pictures I had seen of him in his home. My reaction: I immediately passed out face down on the floor, a common reaction according to the staff on hand. Once revived, I agreed to confirm the identity of the soldier and support the funeral director's call for a closed casket. Thankfully, the family accepted that recomm-endation.

I should mention here that shortly after this notification, in the early summer of 1966, the presumed remains of Navy Corpsman Mark V. Dennis, thought to have been killed in a Marine CH46 Sea Knight (*Chinook*) transport helicopter crash near the North Vietnam / South Vietnam border, were shipped stateside to the Dennis family and buried without visual identification by the family due to the terrible condition of the body. Questions as to the validity of the identification arose almost immediately thereafter and received national press coverage causing great and ongoing anguish to his family and friends who had reason to suspect that he may have been captured and placed in an enemy POW facility. Those concerns were finally put to rest, but not until DNA testing *fifty years later, in 2017,* confirmed that the remains were indeed those of Navy Corpsman Dennis.

As you can well imagine, that note of uncertainty came to affect every notification from that point forward, at least until the bodies were returned home some three weeks later for positive visual identification. That it happened only once and that there were extenuating circumstances surrounding it made no difference whatsoever in the eyes and minds of every next of kin. The constant refrain, regardless of the soldier's family background, education, or color was always the same, "Maybe it's not really my boy in there after all. They do make mistakes, you know." One thing for sure, that one well-publicized story played havoc with the families and made my daily interim visits to their homes quite a bit more challenging. Without fail, someone in the home would greet me at the door with those thoughts and, frankly, I felt like a heel for not encouraging their optimism. Nevertheless, I also knew that I would have felt much worse had I done so, with 99.9% certainty that another mistake had not been made. Thankfully, the funeral directors with whom I worked, fully understood the heightened sensitivity of the bereaved families and went to great lengths to reassure them that proper identification had been made, pre-DNA, of course.

Fortunately, that mistake in identification had not yet occurred, so at least this family was spared that extra degree of angst. The parents had already spent considerable time deciding on the memorial services they wanted for their son, so the final details were implemented quickly, setting the stage for a two-day wake followed by a funeral at the Emanuel AME (African Methodist Episcopal) church in downtown Charleston, one of the oldest black churches in the South, a beautiful church affectionately known as "Mother Emanuel".

On the morning of the funeral, I considered wearing my basic greens, the standard uniform for a memorial service, but instead opted for the more formal dress blue uniform thinking it would present a more professional image in the eyes of family and friends. Once dressed and following a quick breakfast, I headed off to the funeral home at 0800 hours, two hours ahead of the start of the scheduled services. It was a typical early spring day for Charleston, warm and sticky with a slight drizzle. The family gathered at the funeral home with their pastor for some final prayers and then we all headed off to the church, which was packed by the time we arrived. Not surprisingly, everyone was dressed in their Sunday finest, making me very happy that I had opted for my dress blues. The soldier's mother asked me to sit on a stool to the right of the casket facing the mourners and then asked that I offer a few words about her son towards the end of the service, a request I had not expected, and one which required some quick thinking on my part.

What, I wondered, would be the best way to reach out to the men and women sitting directly in front of me, all of whom I assumed had a long-term relationship with the soldier? Obviously, my role dictated that I focus primarily on his military service which certainly posed no problem whatsoever since I knew that he was a decorated war hero. But what could I say to bridge the very obvious gap between me and the congregation? Clearly, I needed to begin my reflections with something subtle but powerful enough to pique their curiosity. But what could that be?

As I looked out at all the distraught faces, I was suddenly struck by the contrast: me a white Army officer from up North, facing and about to deliver a eulogy to an all-black Deep Southern congregation burying one of their own. And then, out of the blue, the obvious answer hit me, an opening sentence simply reflecting what I was thinking as I sat there.

So, when my time to speak arrived, I stepped up to the pulpit, looked out over the hundreds of grief-stricken faces, cleared my throat, and spoke from the heart: "I envy all of you." That one sentence started a very vocal mumbling within the church, men and women looking at each other and clearly saying, "Did he just say that he envies *US*?" I continued, "You had the opportunity to know this brave soldier, many of you for his entire life. I did not. You experienced his warm personality, his great sense of humor, and his love of life. I did not. You were also there to share in his many athletic and scholastic achievements. I was not. I am thankful; however, for being given the opportunity to learn about him through conversations with many of you over the past several weeks and by reflecting upon his positive accomplishments during his all-too-brief Army career. He was special, no doubt about it, a true hero with the Bronze Star to prove it, and although his time among us was far too brief, our memories of him will remain with all of us for the rest of our lives. May he rest in peace."

Immediately following my brief comments, and just as the emotions throughout the congregation were beginning to subside a bit, a woman came racing up the center aisle of the church literally screaming at the top of her lungs, "Come on out of there, boy. You ain't really dead." She then started furiously pounding on the lid of the closed casket with both fists. My first thought was, "Oh my God. Who is she and how did she get in here?" My immediate concern: would she actually try to open the casket which, considering the poor condition of the body, would have been disastrous on so many levels. Yes, I was right there next to her, but I couldn't imagine what I could or would do if she made that move. Fortunately, she did not, apparently content to wail away while pounding on the lid, driving the mourners into an absolute frenzy. Interestingly enough, the funeral director was also close by, on the opposite side of the casket, yet he seemed completely unconcerned by her actions. Puzzling for sure, but also somewhat reassuring that things would not spiral out of control. After several minutes of chaos, relative calm was restored but only when the Honor Guard, on my discrete hand signal, marched to the front of the church and carried the casket down the aisle and out the back door followed closely by the woman and her non-stop plea for the soldier to wake up.

What I did not know at the time was that the woman was a regular presence at many black funerals in the area. This I discovered the following day when I went back to the funeral home specifically to ask the funeral director to please, *please* make every effort to keep her away from any Army funerals. He looked at me, smiled, asked me if that had been my first black funeral, reached into his file cabinet, and pulled out a copy of his funeral check list pointing to Item #17, "Official Mourner" at a cost of $20. That woman and I were destined to meet numerous times at other funerals within the black community, and at one point I asked her how she viewed her role in a memorial service. Her response surprised me but in its own way it did make perfect sense. "You're here representing the Army, to talk about the war and the boy's military service to his country. I get hired to bring a higher level of emotion to the service. What I do allows the mourners to let go of their inhibitions, let it all out one last time, which really seems to help them cope with their loss. Think of me as the grand finale of a fireworks show." From that day forward I noticed that her mere arrival at any funeral caused quite a stir among the mourners. They knew they were in for a dramatic and emotional experience and she never let them down.

The trip to the cemetery took less than a half hour, and the graveside service, complete with full military honors provided by an Honor Guard Unit from Ft. Jackson, was brief and dignified, ending with my presentation of the folded American flag to the soldier's parents. The remaining paperwork was completed over the next several weeks and was followed by a special ceremony at the Army Depot at which time Colonel Campbell presented the parents with both the Bronze Star for bravery and the Purple Heart, awarded to military personnel wounded or killed in the line of duty in a combat zone.

This pattern became the basis for all of my earlier Casualty Notification/Survivors Assistance cases leading me to believe that I had a solid handle on that critically important part of my new assignment. In hindsight, however, I soon discovered that, although the majority of the cases generally followed a similar pattern, each one, in its own way was unique, requiring individualized attention and flexibility. In addition, I also realized that I needed to have a better understanding of Southern black culture and traditions.

CHAPTER 4

The Ugly Face of Prejudice:
The emotional landscape of the 1960s Deep South.

Professional mourners, the Ku Klux Klan, the "War of Northern Aggression", black culture – Southern style, totally segregated public schools more than a decade *AFTER* the iconic Brown vs. the Board of Education ruling, the mystical Gullah/Geechee language and culture, "brass ankles" – the list goes on and on. So much I needed to learn about the people of South Carolina, black and white alike, now that I realized I would be working directly with them on a daily basis. What had I learned up to that point? Well, chronologically, the first thing that had struck me upon my arrival in Charleston on that early March evening of 1965, was the relationship of blacks to whites. The white folks were clearly in charge and the black folks seemed to accept that reality without visible complaint. Quite a contrast to the environment I was familiar with in New York. To the casual observer, it was probably not even that noticeable at first, yet there it was, and it was clearly present across most levels of southern society. Was the aura of prejudice always that subtle throughout the Deep South back in those days? It was not. How could I ever forget the enormous sign with five-foot-tall individual block letters positioned crescent-shaped across the entire front lawn of a motel on the west side of U.S. Highway 301 in Fayetteville, North Carolina proudly proclaiming: **N-O C-O-L-O-R-E-D-S**. That said, any remaining subtleties that I may have seen in my day-to-day life certainly vanished into thin air in the late winter of 1965-'66, as a result of that request from Colonel Campbell that I go as a "prospective new recruit" to a Ku Klux Klan rally near Charleston. The colonel was relatively new to the area, having recently been transferred from an Army post located deep in another southern enclave, Anniston, Alabama, and he wanted objective feedback on the degree of hostility toward blacks at his new posting. It would prove to be an eye-opening experience for me.

The assignment came about as a result of the colonel's friendship with one of the senior civilian employees in the Depot's engineering division. Through that relationship, he learned that the gentleman was a longtime member of the local Ku Klux Klan chapter in his hometown of Summerville, a medium-sized community about 25 miles north/northwest of Charleston. Over the course of several months, he had attempted on numerous occasions to convince Colonel Campbell that the violence attributed to the KKK was not only ancient history but, even then, grossly exaggerated, and that he should go with him to a meeting to see for himself. Clearly, as the highest ranking active duty Army officer in the Charleston area, the colonel didn't feel that he could accept such an offer, tempting as it might be, so by default he recruited me in his place, assuring me that "my friend will be with you if things get uncomfortable." Not particularly reassuring words, but the request from the colonel wasn't really a request, so I cancelled my plans for the evening and listened to his instructions.

The plan was simple. I would drive to Summerville shortly after work to be briefed on what to expect and instructed on basic KKK protocol. I would be introduced at the start of the rally as a possible new recruit from Virginia, technically correct in that I had recently arrived in Charleston following my nine-week officer training course at Ft. Lee. The invitation came, they would be told, because of my interest in learning more about the goals and objectives of their chapter first-hand; sort of comparison shopping on the focus and goals of one state's chapter versus another's.

I arrived in Summerville at 1800 hours and was

welcomed by my host for the evening and introduced to his wife, Elizabeth, who had prepared a delicious meal of chicken purlieu, macaroni and cheese, and collard greens, topped off with my first slice of homemade key lime pie. No doubt about it, I was quickly becoming addicted to southern cooking. Less than ninety minutes later, we were off to the rally just a short distance away, with me riding shotgun in his pickup truck. This promised to be an interesting evening for me: twenty-four years old, a lifetime Yankee, heading off to mix and mingle with a group of men with backgrounds very different from mine. Not to mention, I assumed, with very different philosophies on life and how it should be lived. So, although I had no idea what to expect from the evening, I knew that at the very least it would be a unique experience. It certainly was that, and then some. I wasn't really concerned for my own safety, assuming that even if they disliked me, which was certainly possible, the worst-case scenario would most likely be a "request" that I leave, a "request" that I would have had absolutely no problem honoring.

When we arrived at the site off a local back road, I saw a crowd of several dozen mostly middle-aged men plus a few younger ones looking to be barely out of their teens, virtually all of whom also seemed to have arrived in pickup trucks. The weather was typical for the season and for the time of day, cool and moist. The men were casually dressed, most in jeans and long-sleeved work shirts. No white robes, conical hoods, or masks as I more or less expected. Apparently, no reason to hide their identity among friends and no need for intimidation out there in the woods. They were mostly gathered in small groups, although a surprising number, myself included, were simply watching from the perimeter. Eventually, the meeting started to take shape and I was introduced to the group as a possible recruit from Virginia now transplanted to South Carolina and interested in learning how their objectives compared to those I was presumed to be familiar with in southern Virginia. I nodded, smiled, and waved to them but kept my comments to a very few carefully crafted sentences, all spoken in my halting version of a newly acquired southern drawl.

"Thank ya Woody. Nice to see y'all. I'm alookin' forward to hearin' about your plans for this part of the country. I also gotta say I'm alovin' Charleston and after samplin' Miss Elizabeth's home cookin' tonight, I'm also alovin' your food. Just gotta get used to the serious deep-fryin' y'all like so much down here, much more so than what I'm used to back up there in Virginia."

Not sure how many people I fooled with that effort, probably not many, but at least I didn't get tossed out on my butt!

Once they had moved past hearing me out, they introduced one other recruit, about my age who, without a doubt, instantly qualified as a perfect fit for the KKK. His opening comment, "The problem with niggers nowadays is that they just don't know their place anymore. They are constantly being riled-up by the God-damned N-A-A-C-P, an anti-American bunch if ever there was one. Those sons o' bitches are just trying to destroy our country and our traditions and we can't let 'em get away with it! They're poisoning the minds of all the niggers, telling them they are equal to us! Can you believe that? Now for God's sake, have you ever seen or talked to even one nigger who was even close to equal to you? Of course you haven't! And you never will! Men, it's our God-given right and responsibility to keep 'em all in their place!" Not surprisingly, those comments drew many loud and enthusiastic "Amens" from all. For that night at least, I was very happy to have placed a distant second in oratory.

From that point forward, the agenda for the evening was quite informal, floating from topic to topic but with very pointed messages delivered throughout. At one point, for example, the talk turned to identifying with the goal of "outing" to use a more recent expression, any and all "brass ankles" in the area. Of course, I had no idea what a "brass ankle" was, but it obviously was a derogatory expression aimed, I assumed, at the black population. The overall tone of the comments made during the evening were pretty much in line with what I had been told to expect. In other words, no specific threats of violence although there were certainly large pockets of raw hatred everywhere, directed at "the uppity blacks from the North, the two-faced white liberals from the North, the money-grubbing Jews, and anyone else who tries to interfere with our way of life."

I managed to stay pretty much in the background throughout the meeting, speaking at length only to my host and briefly to one other individual who approached me midway through the evening saying, "I know you. You're that new lieutenant at the Depot! I didn't realize that you were a southern boy. Nice to see you here supporting our cause." I had never laid eyes on him, but I later discovered that he also worked in the engineering division. Fortunately, he was a pretty low-key guy and seemingly more amused than anything else to see me there.

When the rally ended about an hour and a half before midnight amid raucous cries and shouted pledges to keep the long-standing traditions of the South alive, most of the men loaded into their trucks and headed back down the road with horns blasting. The officers of the chapter, however, had other plans. For them, the evening had only just begun. Since I was a guest of one of those officers, I was invited to join them at a small cabin just a short distance away, the best way, I was assured, to get "a complete picture of the KKK." There the men would gather to review the evening's activities and begin planning for the next event. I was also told that I would enjoy meeting some of the leaders in a more laidback environment and, with a wink, seeing the "fun side" of the Klan. Hmm, the "fun side" of the Klan. Who knew!

The cabin, used primarily during the hunting season, was quite small, sparsely furnished, and generally in poor shape. Describing it as rustic would be a stretch. Homemade moonshine was the drink of choice for most of the men although they did have a couple six-packs of Pabst Blue Ribbon beer available for the light drinkers. I opted for a Pabst. Overall, the mood was festive, thanks in no small measure to the rave reviews the other new recruit was receiving. Not surprisingly, no mention was made of my qualifications, at least none that I heard. That said, a number of the men did spend time with me, focusing their questions on my perception of the mood of the group up in Southern Virginia, looking, I felt, for confirmation that the goals and attitude of that chapter matched theirs. Not easy to bluff my way through that minefield but with my host's help, I escaped relatively unscathed. On my own, I'm virtually certain that I would have been burned at the proverbial stake!

Next up was the main attraction, announced in just that manner, the screening of several very low-quality, well-worn 8MM black & white stag films featuring low-energy white women of average looks and on the plump side engaged in basic missionary style sex with paunchy and not particularly high-energy white men. What I found particularly strange and distracting about the films were the women's feet. "What's with those feet", I found myself thinking? The bottoms of all the women's feet were very dirty. Why, I thought, hadn't they washed them before the action started? After all, thanks to the camera angle, the soles of their feet were closest to the camera. Very odd, I thought and also a bit of an indictment on the supposedly erotic nature of the films. In a perfect stag film, I suspect that I might not have been so fixated on the women's dirty feet.

After lots of hootin' and hollerin' during those

shows, it was time for the grand finale, yet another even lower quality, well-worn stag film with a far different message. Front and center on the screen was a very naked and very well-endowed black man preparing to engage in a romp with a very frightened white woman. "Gentlemen, this is what will happen to us should the niggers ever take control of our lives. Surely, you don't want him having fun with your wife or daughter, now do ya'? We simply cannot let that happen. It is our God-given right and duty to hold onto our traditions and values for our sake and for the sake of all those God-fearing men and women who will follow us. *BEWARE AND BE VIGILANT AT ALL TIMES!*" That said, it was time to head back to my host's home, pick up my car and return to Charleston.

On the ride back, his first words to me were, "So, what do you think? Just a bunch of good ole' boys looking to have some fun, right? No talk of a lynching, hell, not even a threat of a 'good ole' fashioned beating'" he chuckled. "Just like I've been telling the colonel, those stories you read about us in the liberal press are nothing but pure bullshit. All we are trying to do is maintain the lifestyle handed down to us by our parents and grandparents and then pass that lifestyle on to our children and grandchildren. Nothing wrong with that, right?"

Not sure how I should respond to those comments without running a serious risk of forever alienating my fellow employee, so I quickly changed the subject, asking him, "What in the world is a 'brass ankle'?" He looked at me, momentarily stunned. "My God, George, I'm glad you didn't bring that up with one of the men at the cabin." Apparently, as a Virginian, I would have been very familiar with the expression. He explained that "a "brass ankle" is a mixed-race, black-white person who may look like us but isn't. You can tell if they have nigger blood in them if their ankles are noticeably darker than their overall skin color." From the talk at the rally, it was clear that the area had a significant number of "brass ankles" who, once identified, were to be avoided by all self-respecting white folks.

The following morning, I was called into Colonel Campbell's office for a debriefing on my night with the KKK. I described the evening as quite an eye-opener for me, a baptism by fire into the thought process of those men who were supporting and encouraging institutions such as the KKK. The colonel was not surprised to hear my comments, adding that "as a native of Tennessee, I grew up surrounded by that attitude and learned over the years how to deflect it from my thought process. Unfortunately," he concluded, "I guess the attitude here is not much different than it was in Alabama." Bottom line: at least in that narrow band of extreme racial hatred, conditions hadn't changed much, if at all, since the end of the Civil War.

What made the whole experience utterly fascinating from my perspective was my background and vantage point. Here I was, a Yankee who had previously never ventured into the South except to visit college classmates living in suburban Arlington County, Virginia, now living in the Deep South and employed by the fully integrated military at an Army depot with only a handful of military personnel and a very large and 100% Southern civilian work force. It made for some very interesting dynamics. Cultural clashes were few at the Depot but inevitable. A perfect case in point: the lieutenant in charge of our Finance & Payroll Division completed his tour of duty and was scheduled to be replaced by a new lieutenant assigned by our headquarters at the Pentagon. Shortly before his scheduled arrival, Colonel Campbell received his Military Personnel 201 file which he forwarded to my office for processing.

Almost immediately, the rumor mill moved into high gear. To this day, I have no idea how word leaked out that the new officer was not only black but a black man from New York City, but leak out it did, and within hours the entire staff of the Finance and Payroll Division, eight or nine middle-aged white women, had signed a petition declaring that, "As God is our witness, we will quit our jobs rather than work for a colored man." They then placed the petition on the colonel's desk and when he returned from his noon meal and saw it, he became enraged and called the entire group into his office. At the meeting, his tone was firm, his Tennessee drawl at full volume, and his message crystal clear: "You will not quit your jobs and furthermore, as employees of the United States Army, you will treat the new officer with the civility and respect that his rank demands."

The new officer arrived at the Depot the following Saturday morning and, as the Duty Officer, it was my responsibility to welcome him to his new assignment. My immediate impression of him was positive. He seemed calm and low-key as did his wife, who had driven down from New York with him. I did notice something strange; however, as I was talking to them: their car was loaded down with a large number of gasoline cans both in the backseat and in the trunk. His explanation was simple: "This is our first trip south of the Mason-Dixon line. We heard stories from friends and neighbors that not all gas stations in the South would serve us. This was also confirmed by the Green Book, which we scanned before leaving New York."

"The Negro Motorist Green Book," a guide for blacks travelling through racially segregated areas of the country, was first published in 1936 by Victor Hugo Green, a postal worker living in New York City, as a guide for blacks wishing to safely travel to a job or go on vacation, with a particular focus on travel throughout the more restrictive Deep South. It offered guidance on a broad range of options available to the black traveler: where you could buy gas / get your car serviced, where you could safely eat or find overnight accommodations, even where you could get a haircut. And, of course, where you could enjoy a beer or glass or wine at a local tavern. It also cautioned black drivers to avoid "sundown towns" – at least 10,000 of them existed during that period, spread throughout the entire country – communities where you were banned at sunset and subject to harassment or arrest for violating the ban. A few towns even had billboards at their borders warning, "Nigger, Don't Let the Sun Go Down on You." Indeed, the unofficial town slogan of one town, located in the southern tip of Illinois, was "Ain't No Niggers Allowed".

Interestingly, the problem was exacerbated throughout the period by the increasing desire of blacks to travel by car. Why the attraction to cars? Largely because it clearly beat the humiliation of being forced to ride in the back of the bus or in the smoky "Jim Crow" car, the first rail car behind the steam locomotive. In addition, the Interstate Highway System, launched in 1956, promised safer roads, away from small town prejudices where it was not out of the question for a black driver to be charged with DWB – "driving while black."

Although passage of the comprehensive Civil Rights Act of 1964 banned such discrimination in all public establishments, change came slowly in parts of the country, in particular throughout a large portion of the Deep South. Nevertheless, the die was cast and "The Negro Motorist Green Book" ceased publication with the 1966 edition. Victor Green's dream, as stated in the 1948 edition, had come true.

"There will be a day sometime in the near future when this guide will not have to be published. That is when we as a race will have equal opportunities and privileges in the United States. It will be a great day for us to suspend this publication for then we can go wherever we please, and without embarrassment."

Bottom line: perhaps the new lieutenant's concerns were indeed valid. Although I had never heard of a local gas station refusing to serve a black customer, I had to acknowledge to myself that it certainly was not out of the realm of possibility, especially in some rural areas.

One thing for sure: their expectations were clearly very modest which certainly helped to make the transition go smoothly. The colonel and I watched with relief and pleasure as the young lieutenant moved effortlessly into his new position the following Monday morning. With the colonel's message still ringing in their ears, the staff treated him with begrudging respect from the get-go and to their credit, quickly grew to realize that black or white, he was more knowledgeable in the finance area than his predecessor and he had a more engaging personality. Barely six months into his job, several of the women who worked for him came into my office and asked me if it would be appropriate to throw a surprise birthday party for him, quite a turn of events and one which gave Colonel Campbell great pleasure.

Through all of this, my perspective was influenced by my New York roots, and importantly, by my almost daily contact with families who had lost a loved one in Vietnam, the majority of whom were black families living either in substandard housing in the poorer neighborhoods of Charleston or way out in the boondocks. In either case, most were subsisting on minimal earnings and living with few modern conveniences. Nevertheless, when the subject of race relations came up, the popular refrain among the vast majority of them was, "This is our home. We're happy here. The white folks, at least the ones we know, tend to treat us just fine as long as we're respectful to them. You know they really do care about us once they get to know us, and they do try to help us whenever we have a serious problem. Our black friends who live up North just don't get that same feeling from their white neighbors. Yes, they tell them that they like them up there but they don't often act like they do."

In all honesty, I probably never fully appreciated that dynamic during those years living in the South but over time, I have come to a better understanding of it. In other words, given the benefit of 20/20 hindsight, it has become clear to me that the general attitude of the white population toward the black population in the Deep South during the tumultuous period of the 1960s was largely relationship based. Clearly, among the better educated white folks, there was often a genuinely protective attitude toward those blacks with whom they had day-to-day contact. In many ways, it seemed almost maternal or paternal in nature, for sure not the best motivation, yet it clearly existed. No question about that. It was an attitude, even affection, that I saw far less frequently among the white population in the North toward their black neighbors. Did the Southerners consider the blacks equal to them in all respects at that time? With very few exceptions, absolutely not! Nevertheless, they tended to be there for them during difficult times and they genuinely grieved with them when one they knew well passed away.

So how did this North/South dichotomy toward blacks come about? Here it helps to step back and examine the overall attitude toward blacks in both environments. In the North, blacks were generally, at least begrudgingly, accepted as being closer to equal than in the South, where the one-hundred-year-old sting of Reconstruction had left an indelible scar on southern society. Bad enough that the "old guard" was forced to deal with the psychological results of the "War of Northern Aggression," they also had to deal with the physical destruction of their beloved land and, perhaps worst of all, they had to contend with despised carpetbaggers from the North, pushing their way into the very fabric of southern society and attempting, often successfully at first, to forcibly re-direct it. Clearly, it was a very bitter pill for those proud people to swallow.

The result was chaotic. Abraham Lincoln's

objective, from the first day of his presidency, had been to keep the country unified. When that effort failed with the start of the Civil War in April of 1861, he adjusted his goal to a reunification of the country. Consider that at the height of the war, in December of 1863, he developed a plan - the 10% Plan - to achieve that goal. Under the terms of his plan, any former Confederate state wishing to rejoin the Union, would simply need 10% of all eligible voters to pledge allegiance to the country and agree to abolish slavery within their state. Congress, however, passed the Wade-Davis bill several months later and it was far more restrictive toward the Confederate states, demanding a 50% pledge of allegiance plus a willingness to sign an oath stating that they had always supported the United States, something most could not do without running the risk of a perjury charge. The Wade-Davis bill also made it much more difficult for those states to establish new governments, something left mostly up to the states under the Lincoln plan. Not surprisingly, the president pocket vetoed the Wade-Davis bill, further infuriating Congress, which countered with the Wade-Davis Manifesto, a blistering rebuke of Lincoln's policies.

Andrew Johnson, who assumed office upon Lincoln's assassination in April of 1865, was no Abraham Lincoln. Far from it. Born in North Carolina in 1808, he was in fact, a serious racist, not at all tuned into public opinion in the North, and totally incapable of dealing with a sharply divided Congress. His first move at the end of the Civil War was to push for new governments throughout the South, governments entirely controlled by white folks. Furthermore, in order to empower those governments, a series of laws, commonly known as "The Black Codes" were adopted in most of those states. These codes granted no civil rights to the blacks, going so far as to make it a crime for a black worker to refuse to sign a coercive labor contract.

TAPS

Congress, led by the Radical Republicans, reacted to those moves by enacting, over Johnson's veto, the Civil Rights Act of 1866, which gave the blacks a number of heretofore unheard of rights - to own property, to compete for jobs in the open market, to testify in court, to sue (and be sued), and to be protected against discriminatory laws such as the Black Codes. They also insisted on new constitutional amendments to guarantee equal rights for all. Merely passing new laws to right the wrong wasn't enough, they argued because, "laws can be struck down with impunity." Not so easy with a constitutional amendment. As a result, the Thirteenth and Fourteenth Amendments, freeing the slaves and granting them citizenship, were drawn up and ratified by the states in 1866 and 1868, respectively. The Fifteenth Amendment, ratified in 1870, extended the vote to all black men. Prior to that time, there was no mention made about the right of black men to vote, granted at that time only by five states, all in the North - Maine, New Hampshire, Vermont, Massachusetts, and Rhode Island, with Iowa and Minnesota following suit in 1868. President Lincoln, as far back as 1863, had believed that all black men who had served in the Union Army - some 180,000 by the end of the war - should be given the right to vote, as should "all black men exhibiting a certain level of intelligence."

The net result of the animosity between President Johnson and Congress culminated with his impeachment in early 1868. Although he avoided conviction by a single vote shy of the two-thirds super-majority needed, his impact from that time forward was severely compromised.

While all of this was transpiring in Washington, the "carpetbaggers" were moving aggressively into the South and working at cross-purposes with the Johnson Administration, getting a significant number of blacks registered to vote which, in turn led to a number of them being elected to political office primarily at the national

45

level. More specifically, and quite remarkably, within the first decade or so following the end of the war, the South had fourteen black men elected to and seated in the House of Representatives and two in the Senate. This led, not surprisingly, to a growing fear among the white population of losing control of their destiny, particularly in those states and districts where they were outnumbered by blacks. How ironic: as slaves, the blacks were kept from obtaining an education by the whites and then, once freed, they were segregated into schools of inferior quality and therefore not qualified in the minds of the white population to hold public office. Not surprisingly, this fear of force-feeding blacks into the democratic process played perfectly into the hands of white supremacists who then created organizations such as the Ku Klux Klan to push back against the black tide.

Meanwhile, back up in Washington, the political tide had once again turned, this time against the initial post-war reforms. President Rutherford B. Hayes in the late 1870s vowed to back off federal efforts designed to support a pro-black interpretation of the Fourteenth and Fifteenth Amendments while at the same time, the United States Supreme Court, in several key decisions handed down between the late 1860s and the mid-1890s did likewise. Indeed, in the 1896 Plessey v Ferguson case, the court ruled that racial segregation was indeed compatible with the Fourteenth Amendment which guaranteed equality before the law. The court's rationale was that "separate but equal" was just fine as long as "equal" was rigorously adhered to, which in practice, it clearly was not. As we know, that decision remained the law of the land until the landmark 1954 Brown v the Board of Education case which concluded that by definition separate could not be equal.

Another decision confirmed that the states were allowed under the Fifteenth Amendment to continue to place "Jim Crow" type restrictive measures such as a poll tax or literacy test on the right to vote even though that Amendment clearly stated that "the right to vote shall not be abridged." By way of explanation, "Jim Crow" was a stereotypical dimwitted black slave created as part of a comedy routine staged by "Daddy Rice," a white entertainer appearing in blackface during the 1820s and 1830s, in some ways a cruder version of Al Jolson singing "Mammy" in blackface or the old Amos & Andy shows of the 1940s & '50s. In the post-Civil War period, the term morphed into a derogatory term describing all anti-black laws put forth during the Reconstruction Period - many well-known laws designed to keep the blacks in check - requiring them to give up their seats or move to the back of the bus, to use only segregated public bathrooms and drinking fountains, and so on. As a result of those actions, the South, in many respects, found itself in the late 1800s to be not far from where it had been before the start of the war in 1861.

Fortunately, I did not personally experience many instances of overt racial prejudice in my day to day job, probably because so much of my work involved working with black families who by their nature tended not to verbalize their feelings on the subject, at least not directly to me. Where I did run head-first into racial prejudice, however, was among a very small number of southern white folks and it was blatant and unapologetic.

My most unpleasant experience during a death notification came in the early summer of 1966. I had received a call from the Presidio late in the afternoon requesting me to notify a woman that her son had been killed in action in Vietnam. Within the hour, I was at the front door of her home in North Charleston, just a stone's throw from the Depot, with the news. The mother, a white woman looking to be in her mid-forties, took the news better than most, obviously fully aware of the risks her boy had been facing on a daily basis. After a general conversation pretty much focusing on steps to be taken down the road, she asked me a simple question: "How many boys from the Lowcountry have been killed in this God-awful war?" I thought a moment and replied, "Approximately twelve up to this point." Next came the troublesome question. "That sure sounds like an awful lot of our boys. You're not counting the niggers, are you?" When I told her I was counting all the soldiers from the area who had died serving their country, she took one look at me and screamed at the top of her lungs, *"**Don't you dare put my son in the same category as those niggers! Don't you dare do that!**"* The power of her rage caught me completely by surprise. In hindsight, it was the only notification I would make where I felt sickened by a next-of-kin's attitude. My challenge going forward was to maintain a total focus on giving her son a proper military sendoff, which he certainly deserved, in spite of my personal animosity toward his mother.

Another example of overt prejudice came from a very unlikely source and as part of a well-intentioned experiment by Colonel Campbell. Realizing by the late summer of 1966 that my job had become close to overwhelming, he suggested that whenever possible, I bring along a local minister to assist in the immediate aftermath of the notification. Certainly, it was a logical idea that made perfect sense. Under Army regulations, I was still responsible for the actual notification but having a man of the cloth there to lend follow-up support to the family could only be a positive, or so we thought. Indeed, one such person, a local minister, who was also a chaplain in the downtown Army Reserve unit, had offered to help out whenever needed. With that in mind, I contacted him and he agreed to go with me on my next notification, which came up several days later.

After I confirmed his availability, I contacted the Depot motor pool to requisition an Army vehicle and driver for the notification. Clark, a black native of Charleston, who would become my right-hand man in virtually all future notifications, picked me up at my apartment and we drove off to pick up the minister at his downtown church. As we headed off to the home of the soldier's family, I took a moment to remind the minister that I would make the actual notification after which he could step in and say some reassuring prayers with the next of kin and family. He assured me that he was well-versed in proper protocol and that he was glad to be of assistance. Off to a good start; however, unfortunately, everything went downhill from that moment forward. Clark made a right turn onto President Street which led to an immediate question from the minister.

"Where are we going?"

When I gave him the address he looked at me and said, *"Whoa! That's in Niggertown. No way I'm going to go on a notification to one of them. No Way!"*

Although by that time, I was quite accustomed to such a reaction by some Southerners, I was absolutely dumbfounded to hear it come from the mouth of an ordained minister, especially in front of Clark. Sadly, Clark was also quite used to that attitude among some Southern whites so he somehow managed to keep his emotions in check. Nevertheless, his tight facial expression and white-knuckle grip on the steering wheel confirmed his anger at the slur. Not about to give up without a fight, I reminded the minister of the scope of his responsibilities especially as an Army chaplain. No dice. He remained adamant in his refusal to do his job.

His only comment to me was, "If you had told me it involved a nigger, I would have saved you the trouble of picking me up."

At that point, I had no choice but to ask Clark to drop me off at the soldier's home to complete the notification, take the minister back to his church, and then return to pick me up.

The following morning, I related the experience to Colonel Campbell who was outraged at the minister's behavior. He did point out, however, that there wasn't much he could do other than place a call to the chaplain's South Carolina reserve unit, which he felt might well play-down the incident. From a practical standpoint, he properly surmised that the last thing I needed was having his help in fulfilling my responsibilities. Issue resolved: I would continue to make all notifications on my own.

On those rare moments when I wasn't covering some aspect of Casualty Notification or Survivors Assistance, I did enjoy at least a taste of the many good things Charleston had to offer: great food, especially seafood, at a variety of quality restaurants, Broadway-quality productions at the Dock Street Theater, and for a total change of pace, a high school football or basketball game. Both sports at that level drew large crowds of rabid fans, especially the Friday night football games.

On one particularly quiet evening, I drove to downtown Charleston to take in a high school basketball game between Charleston High School and Bishop England High School, a prominent Catholic high school, located in the city. The experience was not what I had expected and discouraging. Although the public-school system remained segregated at that time, Bishop England was integrated and they had a black player on their starting five. Within minutes of the opening tip-off, it became patently obvious to anyone with even a rudimentary knowledge of the game that he was the best player on the court, frankly by a wide margin. It also became immediately obvious to me that the fans in the stands, virtually all of whom were white high school students, were experiencing something new and foreign to them: a black player playing in an integrated sporting event in their hometown and on their home court. Sadly, the better the kid played, the more the all-white crowd got on him. Under normal circumstances, had they booed him lustily, I would have been perfectly happy. Why not? That's what fans often do to an outstanding player on the opposing team. But no, following virtually every beautiful pass or fancy drive to the basket, the entire crowd of students stood up, pointed at him, and laughed very loudly. It was so perfectly coordinated that it almost seemed rehearsed. I had no idea at that time what the player must have been thinking but to his credit, he continued to give his best effort throughout the game.

After the game, I felt compelled to walk down to the visitor locker room to talk to him. After introducing myself as an Army officer stationed in Charleston and congratulating him on his play, I mentioned the reception he had received by the crowd. His response – a shrug of the shoulders and a practical reaction:

"I'm getting used to it. My Dad tells me to play right through it and hopefully over time, I'll win over the crowd."

Nevertheless, my thoughts as I drove home that night: this is the upcoming generation. There is still a lot of work to be done.

Finally, I would be remiss if I failed to mention another example of prejudice, in this case directed against me. Make no mistake about it, this incident falls far short of every single one highlighted within this chapter, nevertheless, it had a profound effect on me because it was personal and unexpected.

By the fall of 1965, I had been living in Charleston for about six months and with some time to kill one Saturday evening, I drove to the annual Charleston County Fair which was set up within a few hundred yards of my home in North Charleston, just off Montague Avenue. After treating myself to a few carnival rides and a bunch of snacks, I met a nice girl about my age, and after a very pleasant conversation, asked her if she would like to go to a movie the following Saturday evening, at a theater located right in the neighborhood. She accepted and the date was set. Something to look forward to.

When the evening arrived, I drove the short distance to her home in Berkley Heights, parked my car, and walked up the path to her front door. My knock was quickly answered, not by my date but by a rather severe looking woman, mid-forties, I guessed, with gray hair pulled back tightly in a bun. She introduced herself as Gwen's mother but made no move to invite me into her home. Quite the contrary! With a clipped delivery and steely gray eyes, she proceeded to ask me three questions straight out. First question:

"Are you in the military?" Keep in mind that the military establishment was generally held in high regard in Charleston at that time.

My answer: "Yes Ma'am. I am a lieutenant in the United States Army stationed at the Charleston Army Depot." No response.

Second question: "Are you a Yankee boy?" Now she was moving into more treacherous waters. My answer: "Yes Ma'am. I was born and raised in New York." No response.

Third question: "Are you a Catholic boy?" Now I realized that this date was in serious jeopardy. My answer: "Yes Ma'am, I am."

And my instincts were right. That proved to be the third strike. Her response: "We are strict Southern Baptists and I cannot allow my daughter to go on a date with you."

To put this in perspective, my relationship with the moms of girls I had dated over the years was generally positive. I didn't drink or smoke, I had a solid education, and now I had a respectable job, characteristics which often made me more popular with mom than with my date. So, needless to say, I was devastated, not so much by the lost evening with Gwen, but by the flat-out rejection by her family.

I fully realize that that rejection pales in comparison with levels of prejudice experienced regularly by most minorities to this day, yet it proved to be one of those defining moments in my life that I have never forgotten and it undoubtedly goes a long way toward explaining my strong aversion to prejudice in all its ugly forms.

CHAPTER 5

Dual Trauma:
The tragedy of losing two sons within the same month.

During the earlier years of the Vietnam War it was
not particularly unusual to find more than one family
member serving on the front lines at the same time. From
the military's perspective, it made perfect sense. It just
wouldn't be fair, they reasoned, to deprive a second or
possibly even a third member of a family of the opportunity
to serve on the battlefield. After all, wasn't a combat
posting one of the reasons many joined the military in the
first place? In addition, it was a widely-held belief that
successful front-line experience was a sure-fire path to
faster promotions. The cynical theory was that all branches
of the military were anxious to entice as many volunteers
into uniform as possible, especially as the war became
increasingly more unpopular with the American public. My
guess is that there is some truth in both theories. In either
case, my understanding is that the policy was eventually
modified as the war dragged on, and casualties and protests
mounted.

With that as a backdrop, it was not surprising that
one of my cases, in the late spring of 1966, involved a
soldier killed in Vietnam and accompanied back to the
states by his older brother. Normally, a soldier's body
could be accompanied to its final destination stateside by a
soldier from the same unit completing his overseas tour of
duty; however, where a relative was serving in the same
theater of operations, it was also possible for him to be
selected to fulfill that function. Once a non-family escort
arrived at the final stateside destination, he was instructed
to check in with the soldier's family and, if possible, stay
for the memorial service, particularly if he had a close

relationship with the deceased soldier. If not, he would be instructed to hand off the responsibility to the Survivors Assistance Officer and then use whatever time was left on his leave to visit with his own family prior to heading off to his next assignment.

In this case, a young PFC was killed while on patrol. His older brother, wrapping up his one-year obligation, was authorized to accompany his brother stateside. My notification to the parents had gone as well as could be expected, aided considerably by the fact that both of them were deeply religious. Both were, in fact, serving in the ministries of different black churches located in downtown Charleston.

The days following the notification were spent making plans for the memorial service for their son. Since the parents were part of separate congregations, they asked if it would be at all possible to have two services, the first at the mother's church and the second at the father's. Since their request involved no additional cost to the military, I assured them that it could be done. On the spur of the moment, I also suggested that they might want to consider a walking procession between the churches since they were less than a mile apart, a suggestion that they found very appealing. The schedule would then conclude with full military honors at the family burial plot located behind an old country church on Route 17, about 15 miles north of Charleston.

Not surprisingly, implementing this plan required a somewhat higher level of coordination: the Charleston Police Department would be needed to rope off the procession route between the two churches, and the South Carolina Highway Patrol would be asked to handle the expected heavy flow of traffic between the downtown church and the cemetery, most likely during the late afternoon rush hour. Without exception, both units cooperated fully and enthusiastically with our requests, highlighting a little known reality of the times: in all cases involving military sacrifice, the subject of race was not a factor within the law enforcement community, even in the 1960s Deep South.

Strictly by coincidence, I had been approached by *Life Magazine* a week or so earlier asking if they could accompany me on my next Survivors Assistance case, start to finish, for a story they were working on exploring the largely unspoken reality of the war, namely the toll it was taking on the families of the soldiers. Since Colonel Campbell had previously cleared it with the Pentagon, I called *Life Magazine* and invited the team to Charleston to witness the proceedings firsthand.

The soldier's body arrived back in Charleston on the evening of the 20th day accompanied by his brother. My impression of the brother was very positive. Two years older and exactly my age, he was naturally devastated by the loss of his kid brother but also very concerned about the well-being of his mom and dad. As I drove him from the funeral parlor to his home, I filled him in on the latest developments on the home front and he, in turn, gave me a very helpful perspective on his parents. Clearly, seeing him back home did a world of good for the parents, giving them the shot of adrenaline they would certainly need to help them through the upcoming services.

The weather on the morning of the funeral was ideal: cool, bright and sunny, with low humidity, a good start to what promised to be a very long and stressful day for the family. The first service, two-and-one-half hours in length before an overflow crowd, was highly emotional, ending with a heartfelt eulogy by the soldier's mother. Safe to say that as she concluded her comments there was not a dry eye in the house.

The procession to the father's church took about 45 minutes and it was an incredible sight on so many levels: hundreds of black mourners winding their way through downtown Charleston streets, with the processional route lined on both sides by a large number of white men, women, and children, all respectfully bowing their heads or making the sign of the cross as the flag-draped coffin passed by. Quite frankly, I found it an amazing moment, especially considering the degree of racial unrest throughout the country at that time. Once again, there was only one obvious conclusion: the fallen soldier was from their hometown; therefore, it was totally fitting and proper to pay him respect regardless of his color.

The memorial service at the father's church, also before a packed house, lasted well over three hours and, on an emotional level, matched that of the earlier service, with the father's concluding eulogy beautifully and emotionally delivered. Needless to say, my brief eulogies paled in comparison to those delivered by the parents.

A one-hour drive across the Cooper River Bridge and up Highway 17 put the large group of mourners at the cemetery by late afternoon, giving us plenty of time to complete the military send-off: final prayers, the Honor Guard firing off their salute, Taps, and the lowering of the body as I presented the folded American flag to his parents, a moment captured by *Life Magazine*.

As I was preparing to leave the cemetery, the parents invited me back to their home for a gathering of family and close friends. They indicated that it was important to them for me to spend some time with their other son before he headed off to his new assignment. Naturally, I accepted their invitation, and when I arrived, was amazed at the number of people who were already there. Of course, I shouldn't have been, considering the obvious affection for the family throughout the community. Everyone it seemed, had also arrived with platters of home-cooked food for the occasion. As we ate, the parents took turns telling me and others nearby many stories about their son, the athlete, the musician, and the student.

CHAPTER 5

After dinner, the brother and I drifted off for an hour or so and quickly found some common ground: the state of racial relations in the country and more specifically in the South. Like many blacks from the area, he believed that the white folks treated the blacks, at least those whom they had known for years, with a decent amount of respect, not as equals, but with respect. His thought was, as a starting point, to find a way to expand that level of respect beyond established relationships. I was impressed by his insight and his determination to push peacefully toward that goal. Yes, our backgrounds were very different, yet our goals were aligned. In hindsight, that was unquestionably what his parents had in mind when they extended the invitation to me to join them that evening. I left their home about an hour before midnight and went home physically and emotionally exhausted but satisfied that the day, though difficult, had achieved the goal of a proper military tribute. Tragically, the family nightmare had only just begun.

The following evening, I received a call from the brother, who was scheduled to board a military flight to his new assignment the next day, to thank me for helping his parents through their ordeal and to suggest that we meet again once he returned home. I told him that I would most likely still be stationed at the Army Depot, although an assignment to Vietnam was obviously a possibility. He asked me to keep an eye on his parents while he was away, which I promised to do, and he ended the call telling me that he was off for a quick beer with some of his old high school friends, many of whom I had met at the wake and funeral.

The dreaded call came to me just shy of 0500. My first thought was that it was from the Presidio and that it was several hours later than normal. It was not from the Presidio; however, but from the South Carolina Highway Patrol asking me if I was still the contact point for Army-

related issues in the lower part of the state. When I
confirmed that I was, I was told that the brother had been
killed in an auto accident. The officer then offered to send
one of his men out to bring the news to the parents.

Although the last thing I wanted to do at that
moment was face the parents again with that news, I felt it
was my responsibility to do so. "No," I found myself
saying, "thank you for your offer, but I will bring the news
to the family myself." The officer then gave me the details
of the accident that ended in his death. Although it was
possible that he had consumed a bit too much alcohol in his
attempt to drown his sorrows, it seemed more likely that he
was just totally exhausted from the emotions of the
previous several days. Whatever the reason, he missed a
turn not far from his home and tumbled down a steep
embankment to his death.

The half hour drive to the parents at sunrise that
morning was, without question, the most difficult and
upsetting single moment of my entire tour of duty. Of
course, every notification was difficult since it carried with
it the reality that I was about to shatter the dreams of a
family. Yet, this one was in unchartered territory for me:
facing parents less than 48 hours after they had buried their
younger son, to tell them that his brother had also died.
That I had quickly developed a warm relationship with the
brother added yet another layer of personal anguish to the
notification. Yes, I knew the parents were strong. I had
seen that strength throughout their ordeal; nevertheless, I
was all but certain that this blow would destroy whatever
reserve they had left.

I arrived at their home at just past 0600 and
immediately noticed a Highway Patrol car discreetly
parked around the corner from the family's home awaiting
my arrival. As I pulled up to the front door, I knew full-
well that the combination of their son not returning home
on his last night in Charleston, combined with the sight of

me walking up their front path, would send them over the edge, and it did. Both came racing out of their home with terror in their eyes shouting, "*Oh God, no, no!*" A simple nod of my head acknowledged that their worst fears were realized. All the composure that they had shown during the previous weeks vanished in a split second. Two terrific sons, their only children, and now both gone. There was simply nothing I could have said or done that would have made much of a difference.

I stayed with them throughout the morning while they called relatives and friends and left only when they had a number of those closest to them at their side. Although I visited with them the following day, I did not begin to talk to them about final arrangements until the third day, suspecting that they would request a service matching the one given for their other son, which they did.

The services were identical in all respects and the emotional level equaled the level reached at the previous service. From a personal perspective, my eulogy was unique in that it was the first and only one I would deliver as the Survivors Assistance officer where I actually knew the soldier we were honoring.

With that in mind, I began my talk with, "Normally, I would look out at all of you and mention, as I did a few days ago, that I envied you for knowing him so well. That envy has now been replaced by an acute sense of sorrow simply because I did have the opportunity, albeit an all-too-brief one, to come to know him. During our time together at his brother's wake and beyond, it took us very little time to find common ground in our beliefs and goals in life. He truly loved living in the South and he truly believed that solutions to the problems society now faces in these difficult times are at hand and available to anyone seriously wanting to seek them out. I found him to be a very special human being in every sense of the word, in many ways ahead of his time, and although I will miss him very much, as I know you all will, I do thank God for the time I had with him. One thing I can say with certainty: he will live on in all our hearts for the rest of our lives. May he rest in peace."

At the conclusion of the graveside service, I promised that I would help the parents through the final military paperwork and awards ceremony for both of their sons. At the conclusion of that ceremony at the Depot, which was featured on the local television stations evening news broadcasts, they took me aside and asked that I keep in touch with them while in Charleston, and beyond if possible, a promise I kept during my return visits to the city.

CHAPTER 6

1960s or 1860s?
Way out in the countryside, pockets of the Old South
remained frozen in time.

As my Casualty Notification and Survivors Assistance responsibilities expanded in the summer of 1966 to include roughly 150 miles of the South Carolina coastline, from just south of Myrtle Beach to a few miles north of the Georgia state line, I was authorized access, whenever needed, to an H-13 Huey helicopter based at Ft. Jackson. Why a helicopter? Well, the expanded territory included some rural communities with very limited standard vehicle access. The H-13, a small bubble-domed single passenger aircraft, was capable of flying deep into those isolated areas with ease and, I might add, never failing to cause quite a stir upon landing.

My first call for the helicopter, in the late summer of 1966, led to an unforgettable experience. The soldier's family lived roughly sixty or so miles south/southwest of Charleston and, based on a local road map, a fair distance from anything remotely resembling a paved road. A follow-up call to the nearest State Police Barracks confirmed that the community was indeed deep in the tidal Lowcountry, surrounded on all sides by sprawling plantations and marsh, and comfortably accessible only by four-wheel-drive vehicles. The desk sergeant also volunteered that most of the old-timers living there spoke Gullah/Geechee. "Can't hardly understand a word they are saying."

Clearly, I had a lot to learn before venturing down there the next day. So, after reserving a helicopter for early in the morning, I placed a call to one of the secretaries at the Depot whom I knew lived south of Charleston and near the coast. Even better, she had often spoken to me about the Gullah people. She confirmed the information given to me by the State Police and added some solid historical perspective which proved to be quite useful.

"Yes," she began, "the Africans who arrived in Charleston aboard slave ships in the 1700s from Angola, Sierra Leone, and several other coastal West African countries, were brought here to fill a specific need: to provide free and experienced labor to the rice and indigo plantations of the Lowcountry. Rice was a major crop in our state in those days and those men had been cultivating it back home for generations. Once settled into numerous communities along the coastline from the Carolinas into Northern Florida, they developed their own language as a means of communicating with each other – Gullah or Gullah/Geechee. The new language was an English based Creole, and it includes a rich mixture of various African dialects, a bunch of loanwords adopted in pure form from their native tongues, and an unusual sentence structure. Not easy to understand, especially if they are agitated."

In addition, she mentioned that they mostly lived in close-knit communities, geographically isolated from the mainland white population which historically wanted no part of living in the mosquito infested swamps of the islands, a natural breeding ground for yellow fever and malaria. "That unique isolation," she continued, "has allowed them to retain almost all of their cultural heritage, at least until very recently." She was concerned, however, that encroachment onto their turf, which began in the mid-1950s with the aggressive development of Hilton Head Island as a fancy resort community for the wealthy, would spread and dilute that culture.

And, of course, as we all now know fifty years later, it did just that. Virtually every coastal island with oceanfront beaches, those "mosquito-infested swamps" of the Lowcountry – Kiawah, Fripp, Sea Island in Georgia, and others, have now been turned into luxury resort communities with all the amenities. "Perfect places," she deadpanned, "for you northerners to escape cold winters or enjoy your retirement." The losers in all of this, of course, have been the Gullah/Geechee people and culture, pushed back throughout the second half of the twentieth century in the name of progress. Fortunately, in more recent times, community groups throughout the Lowcountry have banded together with the Gullah/Geechee folks to help preserve this true "Jewel of the Lowcountry" – Gullah/Geechee language and culture, arguably the purest form of black African culture remaining in America.

Historical perspective aside, the secretary hadn't heard that one of the young men had ventured out of his community and joined the Army. She also mentioned that she did not personally know anyone who had any meaningful contact with them, although she did note that perhaps I had seen some of the Gullah women weaving and selling their unique sweetgrass baskets along various Lowcountry roads. Indeed I had. In closing, I asked how she thought they might react to a stranger helicoptered into their midst. She laughed and said, "I have no idea. When you find out, do tell!"

Armed with that fascinating historical snapshot, I drove to the Depot the following morning to await the H-13 which was scheduled to arrive at the Parade Ground at 0730. The pilot landed right on schedule, introduced himself as Captain Donald Hasty, and questioned me about our mission. He had, in fact, recently returned from a year in Vietnam and was looking forward to a new experience which, in hindsight, this would certainly prove to be. Following a brief tutorial on basic helicopter protocol, I took my place in the passenger seat and we were on our way. The quick looping ascent was a new experience for me. Frankly, I also felt like I was wearing the helicopter: it just seemed so small. Captain Hasty indicated that the flight would take about 45 minutes, at which time he would look for a place to land, most likely an open field near the center of the community. My first helicopter flight was pretty amazing, although knowing what lay just ahead, I found it difficult to focus on anything other than the job at hand.

The sight prior to landing was beyond belief: deep in a wooded area and surrounded by very large cultivated fields and swamps, the small community was oriented around a dirt road maybe a couple hundred yards long, flanked on both sides by a number of small buildings, perhaps slightly larger than antebellum slave quarters but not by much. Ambling down the road was a lone vehicle, a small wooden wagon pulled slowly along by a tired-looking mule. Captain Hasty took one look at the scene and mumbled, "I think this is a movie set. Are you sure someone from Hollywood isn't making a Civil War movie down there?" All I could think of was how in the world was I going to communicate with these people now that I had seen first-hand just how isolated they really were. I had been assured that most of them spoke some English, but could I be sure? Obviously, the soldier spoke it, since he had graduated from a local high school and qualified for Army service, but who else could I count on to help me complete my assignment?

My best bet I reasoned, was to find someone who by necessity had contact with the outside world on a regular basis. That was as good a starting point as any and it was my basic objective once I jumped out of the helicopter, which Captain Hasty easily landed in an open field near the center of the community. Fortunately, the answer was right in front of me: a small general store. The store was open and the proprietor, a black man looking to be in his mid-sixties, was friendly and quite fluent in English. He did acknowledge, however, that, "Don't see many strangers in these parts and surely none coming in the way you just did." Fortunately, he did recognize my Army uniform and he was particularly intrigued by the helicopter.

One thing for sure, he knew that I wasn't there to

make small talk and he also guessed, I suspect, that I was there to deliver news about the soldier to his family. He may well have suspected bad news but he didn't ask. He then walked with me down the road, telling me as we walked that it was likely that no one would be home at that time of day as the boy's mother worked in a nearby cotton field.

The family home was a modest but well-maintained wood-frame structure, set back perhaps 40-50 feet from the road. Just looking at the home made me wonder how a young boy who grew up in this isolated environment had somehow ended up in the Army fighting in a war so many thousands of miles from his roots. As I was to later learn from his mother, he was determined to complete high school, no easy feat from that location, thereby making him eligible for the draft which he eagerly embraced, undoubtedly happy for an opportunity to see a bit of the outside world.

As I started towards the front door, painted blue – to ward off evil spirits, I later learned – the next-door neighbor looked over from her front porch and gave me a "what in the world are you doing here" look. I called out the family name, she nodded, and pointed down the road in the general direction of the cotton fields. That walk took about ten minutes, ending at the edge of a very large field populated by a dozen or more black women working away under a broiling mid-morning sun while singing what sounded like an old Negro spiritual. If that wasn't enough of an eye-opener, at the edge of the field a large uniformed white security guard stood watch over the women. It was quite a sight on so many levels.

After digesting that scene for a few moments, I walked over to the guard, introduced myself as a U.S. Army officer and told him that I needed to speak with one of the women on an important Army matter.

His response was less than encouraging: "They get

off work at sundown. It will have to wait 'til then."

That was not the response I had expected and it called for a quick re-evaluation of my position. I certainly was not going to walk away from my assignment and yet I was facing a resistance that I had never before encountered. So, I asked again, stressing that it was a time-sensitive issue that had to be taken care of without delay. Still no movement on his part. He simply reiterated his prior statement and asked me to move on. The die was cast and I knew then what I had to do – locate the soldier's mother on my own. In hindsight, I guess I was counting on the fact that I couldn't really imagine a private security guard, hired by a plantation owner, being foolish enough to threaten or physically restrain a uniformed member of the military there on official business. Fortunately for me, that assumption proved to be correct.

Not surprisingly, by this time all the women in the field were well aware of my presence and, I'm sure, wondering why I was there. I also had to assume that some of them might not speak much English, possibly making delivering my message problematic. With no other option, however, I told the guard that I would locate the woman on my own, figuring that the mere mention of the family name would once again do the trick, and it did. The first woman I approached pointed to another woman several rows over. Sadly, as she saw me coming towards her, she intuitively knew that my visit was not to bring good news about her son and she fell to the ground sobbing uncontrollably. I immediately knelt down in front of her and, mostly through short English sentences and words, confirmed her worst fears.

As sad as that moment was, and it was truly heartbreaking, the reaction of her friends in the field was beautiful and something I have never forgotten. Despite the continuing hostile presence of the guard, they began to quietly call out to her in Gullah, clearly offering words of encouragement. No, they didn't rush to her side; that would have been foolish under the circumstances, but they were brave enough to reach out to her verbally and then, remarkably, they started to sing a different song, led first by those closest to her and then across the entire field. That song, I later learned, dealt with unexpected loss and they sang it with incredible emotion. It was yet another unforgettable moment indelibly etched in my mind.

The next step promised to be a difficult one but one that had to be made nonetheless: taking her back to her home. Clearly, I couldn't leave her out there for the rest of the day in her emotional state, but I also fully expected another confrontation with the guard. When I mentioned the word "home" to her and pointed in that direction, she shook her head vigorously left to right, with fear in her eyes. Nevertheless, I managed to get her on her feet and walking toward the edge of the field, with my right arm around her shoulder. Fortunately for both of us, the guard seemed to have come to grips with the situation and made no effort to restrain us as we passed by his post.

The walk back to her home was difficult on every level: communication was somewhat language-constrained, and the sadness was overwhelming. Fortunately, her next-door neighbor, who had correctly sensed why I was there, had gathered whatever friends were not working in the fields, all of whom rushed to her side as we approached her home, providing her with important emotional support.

While they were consoling the soldier's mother, I walked back to the store hoping to persuade the owner to come back with me to help me explain follow-up procedures to the family. As an incentive, I offered him a ride in the helicopter. Fortunately, he jumped at my offer. Back at the family's home, we spent an hour or so outlining the steps going forward, including a rough timeline before which certain decisions would have to be made. I then walked back to the store and waited while Captain Hasty took the storekeeper up for a short ride, which he thoroughly enjoyed. Interestingly, when they landed, I asked him to pose for a picture in front of the H-13 with Captain Hasty, thinking that he would enjoy showing it to his friends.

He shook his head vigorously saying, *"No, No."*

Why? Apparently, he worried that a picture taken of him could capture his soul.

The period following this particular notification was unlike the others by necessity. Obviously, I could not tie-up an Army helicopter every day, so for the first week, I made regular calls to the store owner who carried messages to and from the family. On my follow-up helicopter visit at the start of the second week, we turned our attention to details surrounding the memorial services, typically routine decisions for the most part, although the isolated location did present some unusual challenges.

Flexibility plus a dose of creativity led to a game-plan covering the basics: selection of the funeral home, church and pastor to preside over the services, cemetery, and of course, the Honor Guard unit to provide the important military touch. I then waited another week for my third visit, at which time I had a confirmed date for the return of the soldier to Charleston, thereby enabling us to set a firm date for the services.

Final arrangements called for a rather unusual single-day memorial program. First up, a late morning funeral at the church, followed by burial with full military honors at a cemetery near the church, and finally a traditional 'home going service' scheduled for the early evening. Family and friends wishing to attend the services were asked to find their way to a staging area off the nearest state road at the edge of the community where they would be picked up and taken by Army buses to and from those services.

On the morning of the services, I drove directly to

the funeral parlor, arriving approximately an hour ahead of the funeral, paid my respects, and headed over to the church, an old wooden structure looking for all the world like every other church sprinkling the countryside in those days. The main difference was that this church conducted some services in Gullah/Geechee. Fortunately, the pastor was also perfectly fluent in English.

When I arrived at the church, I was amazed to see virtually the entire community seated and waiting for the funeral to begin. Quite remarkably, the plantation owner had given all his workers the day off to allow them to support the soldier's family.

The funeral service seemed very similar in structure to many others I had participated in within the black community – Christian-based with a true evangelical feeling. The sermon, in Gullah/Geechee of course, was clearly inspiring to the congregation, although well-beyond my linguistic reach. Ditto for the unaccompanied singing. Familiar sounds from beautiful voices seemingly sung almost in English. I say almost in English since the sounds were familiar as were many of the words, familiar but also different. For example, "Our Lord's Prayer" in English begins, "Our Father who art in Heaven, hallowed be thy name…". In Gullah, the words came out as; "Our Fadduh awt'n Hebb'n, all-duh-weh be dy holy 'n uh rightschus name." A number of other prayers and songs also had a very familiar ring to them.

My eulogy was brief and focused on the young soldier's courageous adventure into the outside world. I did find myself wondering at times if anyone in the church had much of an idea of what I was saying, although I did note that their "Amens" did come at the appropriate time, perhaps thanks to loud "Amens" from the pastor.

The graveside service was similar in most ways to the others I had participated in within the black community with one exception. Before final prayers were spoken by the minister, a drummer circled the grave, a traditional rite, I learned, followed by the mourners singing, dancing, and praying for the family of the deceased soldier. Final prayers were then offered by the minister after which the Ft. McPherson Honor Guard Unit added the rifle salute and Taps.

After a brief respite, the mourners made their way back to the church to prepare for the 'home going service'. Defined as a celebration of a life well lived, it was an amazing contrast to the funeral service just a few hours earlier at the same location. Clearly, this soldier's life was far too short, yet the congregation was able through storytelling, singing, and even light humor, to lift everyone's spirits. After all, their brave soldier was going home to the Lord, reason enough to celebrate. The concept of the obviously contrasting services, I assumed, was to let the family and close friends realize that the deep sadness that they were then feeling for their loss would eventually turn into positive reflections of happy memories with him. It seemed a fitting end to the day.

The final step in our tribute to soldiers killed in the line of duty was, of course, the awards ceremony traditionally held at the Depot and presided over by Colonel Campbell. This proved to be a problem for many of the family, especially for the mother, who seemed very anxious at the thought of the "long journey" to Charleston. Not really surprising considering the almost cloistered nature of her life. When I mentioned this dilemma to the colonel, he suggested that we accommodate both family and friends by having the ceremony within the community with me substituting for him.

In hindsight, having the ceremony at their home proved to be the perfect solution since it allowed the entire family and many of their friends to share in the moment, something that simply would not have been possible in Charleston. I flew down in the H-13 the morning of the ceremony and was pleased to see that the plantation owner had once again thoughtfully given his field hands the morning off from work. Surprisingly, he also came to the ceremony with his young son, standing behind the crowd and telling me afterwards that "He was a fine boy, always respectful to his Mama. I really liked that boy." Once again, another piece of solid evidence that military sacrifice often crossed racial lines even in the 1960s Deep South.

At the ceremony, I read the citations, translated into Gullah on the spot by the family's minister, awarding the soldier the Bronze Star for heroism on the battlefield and, of course, the Purple Heart for wounds sustained in the line of duty. I concluded my comments praising him for leaving the comfort of his home to fight for his country.

Following the ceremony, I was invited to stay for a traditional Gullah meal celebrating his life. And what a meal it was: fresh seafood caught for the occasion, an endless supply of red rice, and a couple of other very tasty dishes, including an interesting one they identified as Frogmore Stew. No frogs in sight! Just a tasty combination of shrimp, corn on the cob, new potatoes, and smoked sausage. Perhaps my imagination, but I'm pretty sure there was also some beer in the pot. All in all, a fitting tribute to a brave soldier and his equally brave family, and a fitting end to a sad but thoroughly memorable experience for me.

TAPS

CHAPTER 7

Learning to Expect the Unexpected:
The importance of a fallback strategy and improvisation.

In reality, every Survivors Assistance case presented a unique challenge of some sort. No two were exactly alike. From the time the case was first assigned to me by the Presidio, most often in the middle of the night, to the final award ceremony presided over by Colonel Campbell, there were always dozens of details to address, many requiring on-the-spot decisions. Yes, many of those decisions became somewhat automatic with experience: the choice of funeral home, the type of memorial service, the advisability of an open casket, the length of the waking period, the level of military honors, and so on. Nevertheless, I simply cannot think of a single case that did not involve at least a couple of unique personal touches that the family desperately wanted to include in the farewell to their loved one. My goal was to accommodate them whenever possible so as to give their brave soldier the best possible sendoff.

In most cases, those requests posed absolutely no problem to me or to the funeral home chosen by the family. Occasionally, however, a request would prove to be a bit of a challenge. A case in point, which will be discussed a bit later: a family's decision to have a two-day wake in their small home, which we reluctantly honored, posed unforeseen problems that clearly would not have happened had the wake been held at a funeral home. That choice was theirs to make and the problems created by it became ours to solve.

In the tragic "Dual Trauma" case, the parents' request for two memorial services certainly posed no problem whatsoever, and my suggestion of a short walking procession between the churches, which did require local police support, proved to be a very special moment for all who witnessed it. Just watching the spontaneous show of sympathy given by the local white population to their fallen black neighbor, was an eye opener for me and also, I am absolutely certain, for many of the black mourners walking through downtown Charleston on that special day.

In the Gullah/Geechee case, the initial challenge focused on finding a way to reach that isolated community and, once there, finding someone to help me communicate with the family. Both the H-13 helicopter and a local translator were essential to successfully completing the assignment and fortunately the H-13 was available to me whenever needed and the on-site translator provided the important link to the community.

In each of those cases, and in many others, a measured degree of flexibility along with a dose of imagination helped to turn requests into reality, much to the relief of the soldier's family and friends. I also quickly learned that Murphy's Law, that old maxim that "If anything can go wrong, it will go wrong," was always lingering just beneath the surface, often leading to last minute glitches that required old-fashioned seat-of-the-pants solutions.

Let's pause a moment and take a look at a few of the glitches that popped-up during my Survivors Assistance work. But before we do, it's important to focus for a moment on the overall environment in South Carolina during the turbulent 1960s. Times were different some fifty years ago, especially in the Deep South. White funeral homes handled funerals for the white folks, black funeral homes for the "colored" folks, and never did either cross the line into the other's territory. More often than not, that divide also held true for cemeteries: white cemeteries for whites, black cemeteries for blacks.

With that as a backdrop, one of the earlier "surprises" during a case popped-up at the very end of what had been a very smooth process, from notification, to wake, and funeral. All that remained was the late afternoon graveside service. The only potential problem was the weather – the entire area was being drenched by a typical mid-summer Lowcountry semi-tropical downpour. Surprisingly, in spite of the miserable weather, a large number of the mourners decided to make the one hour trek from Charleston to Walterboro, about 45 miles west of Charleston. Once they had all gathered at the small cemetery, located adjacent to a small black chapel, it became immediately obvious that not everyone would be able to squeeze inside for the final prayers. Yes, there was a covered portico opposite the entrance which, under normal conditions, would have easily accommodated the overflow crowd.

Unfortunately, conditions were far from normal at the church. The portico was under repair and a large hand-printed sign posted on one of the columns clearly stated:

DANGER!
WEAK FLOOR BEAMS!
CAPACITY LIMITED TO A MAXIMUM OF
10 PEOPLE!

Nothing equivocal about that. My first thought, everything considered, was on the practical side: since the rain had subsided a bit and since most of the mourners were carrying umbrellas, we should move the entire prayer service to the gravesite. The funeral director disagreed. To him, family and friends getting wet was simply unacceptable, so he rationalized that the sign was probably just an overly conservative guess by the contractor, and directed the twenty-five or so individuals standing in the rain to step under the portico roof. To a certain extent, he was right. The floor held the first dozen or so with no problem but then abruptly collapsed as others rushed to secure a dry spot. The result: two dozen men, women, and children were tossed approximately 8-12 feet into a very dark and very wet pit. Judging by the look of panic in the eyes of those still safely above ground, most of them probably had at least one family member in the pit and the shrieking coming from below was frightening.

Fortunately, there was a small parsonage next door to the church from which the minister was able to contact the State Highway Patrol and the local hospital. Thank God also for the Honor Guard unit, which stood ready, willing, and able to help those in the pit, a difficult assignment since many down there were understandably climbing over each other to find a way to safety. The arrival of the police within 10-15 minutes restored order but it wasn't until the ambulances and medical staff arrived that the rescue and triage effort could begin in earnest. By the time a half-dozen or so of the more seriously injured were evaluated and put into ambulances, accompanied by their relatives, over one hour had passed and the crowd had shrunk to a handful of hardy souls, making the final tribute a bit anticlimactic.

On another occasion, and also on a very rainy day, I participated in a funeral about 30 miles northwest of Charleston on the outskirts of Moncks Corner. The burial was scheduled to take place at a small and not particularly well-maintained black cemetery just north of the North Charleston line, between I-26 and the Dual Lane Highway. I had been involved in several other services at that cemetery and I remembered that the ground was solid clay, making grave preparation difficult under ideal conditions. I could only imagine the potential problems during a heavy and sustained downpour. Compounding my concern, it was my first time working with this particular funeral home. Virtually all of my earlier Charleston-based services for the local black population had been coordinated through Fielding Home for Funerals, with whom I had developed a particularly strong relationship and trust.

With the thought of a flooded grave in mind, I

called the funeral director early in the morning and offered
to place a water pump from the Depot at the site to keep it
dry. He thanked me for the call and the offer but assured
me that he was very familiar with the challenges of the
cemetery and that he had devised a solution that he was
certain would eliminate any issues caused by water
accumulation in the grave.

Truthfully, his assurance did little to assuage my
concerns; however, he was in charge and he certainly knew
the cemetery far better than I, so I was left with nothing but
a ton of worries as I sat in the church listening to the rain
pelt down on the roof. What solution did he have in mind, I
wondered, not involving a pump that could possibly work?
I simply couldn't imagine. In any event, the church service
was beautiful, the eulogies by family and friends were
touching, and all that remained was the 45-minute drive to
the cemetery for the final prayers. Unfortunately, that drive
only served to highlight the severity of the storm and
increase my concerns over what we were likely to
encounter once we arrived on site. Fingers crossed and
prayers said, the moment of truth finally arrived. The
"solution" made me want to either cry or laugh out loud.
All I could think of to say to Clark was, "He can't be
serious." He shook his head saying, "That will flat-out
never work."

How to describe the "solution"? Well, for old-
timers, I would bring up the image of Rube Goldberg
"doping it out". For those not familiar with that expression,
I can best describe the "solution" as a contraption which
may have somehow looked theoretically sound on paper,
but which certainly did not look plausible in the field. In
brief, the grave was filled to the brim with water. "Not to
worry" the funeral director assured me after seeing the look
on my face. The "solution" consisted of a five-foot tall
wood- framed structure straddling the grave. "The casket
will be tied to the structure during the final prayers and

military honors, at which time I will cut the rope and the casket will drop perfectly into the grave, expelling all the rainwater off to the far side and away from family and friends sitting nearby." Seriously?

Unfortunately for all, my skepticism proved correct. The final prayers were spoken by the minister, the Honor Guard added their always touching military salute, the rope was cut, and the troubles began in earnest. The casket plunged head-first into the grave throwing mountains of water not to the far side of the grave as planned but directly onto the family sitting at graveside, absolutely drenching them. This quite understandably led to a new wave of turmoil among those at the service while at the same time posing a new set of challenges for the funeral director: getting the casket out of the grave, quickly accomplished by the Honor Guard unit; sending the mourners back to their cars; moving the casket to the small canopy put up for the family; opening it and re-positioning the body; and finally, resuming the service in front of some very wet and anxious mourners.

[As a post-script, a Depot pump was brought on-site after the service was completed to drain the grave prior to final burial.]

One final example, which was clearly the most challenging on several levels. The family of the soldier lived in a black neighborhood in downtown Charleston and the family's church, where we scheduled the funeral service, was just a few miles from their home. The catch: the family cemetery was located behind a very small country church some 60 miles west/southwest of Charleston on Highway 17, several miles outside Ridgeland. No obvious problem. I had previously coordinated a number of funeral and burial services at roughly that distance with ease.

The first hint of a potential problem arose during my call to the Honor Guard unit at Ft. Jackson. The captain in charge of the unit listened to my request and promised to get back to me within 24 hours. Not an unusual response on the surface, but one which I should have questioned. Why? Simply because all previous requests to him had been approved on the spot. Nevertheless, not able to imagine why this request was any different, I fully expected to receive a positive response the following day. I did not get one. Rather, I was told that because the cemetery was so far to the south of the site of the funeral in Charleston, I would need to line up an Honor Guard unit from another Post to cover the burial. His logic was simple yet frustrating. Yes, Ft. Jackson could easily handle the funeral service in Charleston and would be happy to do so, but their Post regulations did not authorize one of their Honor Guard details to travel into the geographic territory of another Army post. In fact, the cemetery was within the operating region of Ft. McPherson, in Savannah, Georgia.

Not a problem I thought. I had utilized the services of the Ft. McPherson Honor Guard unit on several occasions in the past and they had always done an outstanding job. A quick call to them confirmed that they were available for the assignment. So, I now had two units committed to the memorial services, an Honor Guard squad in Charleston, and a chaplain and squad plus a bugler to handle the burial services at the cemetery.

On the day of the funeral, everything went very smoothly in Charleston right through the church service. All that remained was the long drive down Route 17 and the graveside service. The weather was perfect, the drive smooth, and, as a result, we arrived on site in just over one hour's time. Although the Ft. McPherson Honor Guard unit had not yet arrived, I saw no reason for concern. After all, I had re-confirmed their commitment to the assignment earlier that morning and we were about a half hour ahead of schedule.

Fortunately, the funeral home had brought four men

to the site to handle the actual post-service burial so, as a first step, they removed the casket from the hearse and placed it at the grave. Still no sign of the Honor Guard or, for that matter, the Army chaplain who was scheduled to deliver the final prayers. The problem I faced was simple, yet almost impossible to solve: the nearest public telephones were miles away in Ridgeland and, of course, we were decades away from the advent of the cell phone. In other words, I had absolutely no way of knowing if and when the detachment would show up and, in the meantime, more than 100 mourners who had made the long trip from Charleston were standing around waiting for something to happen. This was definitely the time for some creative thinking.

A partial solution involved my trusted driver, Clark, whom I knew was an ordained minister in a small black Protestant sect headquartered somewhere in North Carolina. I also knew that he always carried the Bible and other prayer books with him to read while waiting for me in his car. So, I walked over to him, put my arm around his shoulder and smiled. He looked up at me and said only two words, "Oh, Lord", to which I replied, "You're hired." Fifteen minutes later, with still no sign of the Ft. McPherson crew, we began the service with Clark assuming his new role, a role which he played perfectly, first reading some inspiring and totally appropriate words from his prayer book and then dramatically closing the book as he gazed up to the heavens. All that was left was the rifle salute and the playing of Taps as the body was lowered into the grave. It was at that point that my luck ran out – but only partially. Obviously, there was no Honor Guard to fire the salute or a bugler to play Taps. As I watched the casket being lowered into the grave; however, I heard the unmistakable sound of Taps in the distance. How was that possible? Was my imagination playing tricks on me? Not at all. Once again, Clark had come to the rescue. Unknown to me, he had walked off into the woods behind the small cemetery while I was talking to the soldier's parents and positioned himself perfectly to play the solemn tribute, quite well I thought, on his **kazoo**, the unique sound of which I can still hear to this day. Talk about creativity!

As we prepared to leave the cemetery, the soldier's father came up to me, put his arm around my shoulder and said, "Sir, I give you and your partner credit for pulling it off. You get an 'A' for effort." Clearly, he was not fooled by the substitution, but fortunately he was very understanding. When I reported that aspect of the service to Colonel Campbell, his comment was, "I would expect nothing less from you and Clark."

All in all, considering the large number of funerals we handled, such incidents were very rare indeed, yet when they did surface, they certainly posed unique challenges, challenges that needed to be met quickly so as to minimize the significant degree of anguish to family and friends.

CHAPTER 8

The Purple Heart?
It seemed like a combat zone.

By the end of the hot and humid summer of 1966, my caseload had grown much larger than either Colonel Campbell or I had anticipated. Indeed, I often found myself juggling up to a half-dozen cases simultaneously. Yes, many were Survivors Assistance cases for retired veterans, but an increasing number were active duty cases for soldiers killed in the line of duty. Hardly surprising considering the dramatically increased level of military activity throughout the war zone.

Adding to that dynamic, many of my new cases were well outside the Charleston metropolitan area, requiring substantially more travel time which, in turn, left precious little time to resolve inevitable last-minute "surprises." My general approach to planning each day was mandated by Army rules and regulations plus, of course, a dose of common sense. Top priority was always given to initial notifications, followed by wakes and funerals, and then follow-up visits to families awaiting the return home of their loved one, with those visits prioritized starting with the most recent notifications. Survivors Assistance for retired soldiers, never as complicated or time-sensitive, were scheduled around my active duty obligations.

A prime example of a case requiring a dose of common sense arrived at my office in the final week of August. I was completely booked for the following day with a mid-morning funeral at a small country church roughly 60 miles north of Charleston, just west of Georgetown, followed by afternoon visits to two families awaiting the return of their sons. A full day by any measure; nevertheless, I was certain that, barring any last-minute surprises, I would be able to stay on schedule. Silly me! By that time, I should have realized that surprises were increasingly becoming part of my daily routine.

In any event, and in anticipation of that busy day ahead, I planned to spend a quiet evening at home: eat a nice meal, watch some television, and get a good night's sleep. With that in mind, I stopped by a local fish market after work and bought a nice fresh swordfish steak, my favorite seafood. Fresh swordfish, dipped in whole milk for 15 minutes, covered with crushed cornflakes to hold in the moisture, grilled over a charcoal fire, and sprinkled with fresh lemon juice. Hard to beat that. To top off the evening, I planned to eat in front of my television watching "Bonanza" in beautiful living color. For those not yet fifty years old, I'm sure it's difficult to imagine the pure thrill of seeing a television show in color, and no one did it earlier or better than "Bonanza". Also, in those days prior to videotapes, DVD's, or any of the other "on demand" technologies available today, if you missed the initial screening, which I had, you were forced to wait months for the summer reruns.

Unfortunately, those carefully made plans went up in smoke, so to speak, shortly after 1900 hours, just as I lit my outdoor grill, courtesy of a call from the Presidio requesting that I notify a mother of the death of her son. Under Army regulations, I had two hours before the 2100 hour evening deadline to make the notification. Theoretically, assuming Clark was available on short notice, I saw no problem in getting to the family's home in downtown Charleston comfortably ahead of that deadline. A call to his home confirmed his availability, so I dressed in my uniform and awaited his arrival.

Of course, I did have another option: to put off the notification until the morning on the theory that I just might be cutting it too close to the deadline. So, why not finish my dinner and get a good night's sleep? Tempting for sure, but not a good choice. Why? Well, for one thing, experience had proven, time and time again, that it was impossible for me to get a good night's sleep with a notification hanging over my head as was so often the case thanks to those late-night calls from the Presidio. More to the point, my schedule was already booked solid with the long drive up Route 17 for the morning funeral. Yes, I could have made the notification right at 0600; however, that would have given me precious little time to stay with the next of kin and family, to me an extremely important part of the post-notification process. To simply make the notification and then bolt out the front door was never an option in my mind. Experience had shown me that an hour or two with the soldier's family, immediately following the notification, really helped them as they moved forward with their grim preparations.

A second factor to consider: experience had also clearly shown that, although most of my notifications were assigned to me after midnight thereby requiring morning visits to the next-of-kin, afternoon or evening notifications tended to work better simply because more family members were at home at the end of the day and therefore available to provide a stronger support system for the next-of-kin. Yes, in many instances, neighbors did their best to be supportive; but, at a time like that, family ties were unquestionably of the most value.

Clark arrived right on time and, as we headed downtown, he warned me that the neighborhood we were going to was one of the rougher ones in Charleston. Certainly not rough or dangerous by big city standards, but clearly more than a bit dicey in those racially-charged times. Yes, I felt safe in my Army uniform and vehicle, but I also realized that this particular visit, on a hot and humid late August night, had an element of risk I had not yet experienced.

Clark located the soldier's home with no trouble, putting me well within the 2100 hour deadline. As I walked up the short front path, I noticed a woman, whom I assumed to be the soldier's mother, looking at me through a side window. No need to knock on the door. She threw it open as soon as I reached it, perhaps just surprised to see a white guy in her neighborhood at that time of night. For sure, she did have an anxious look on her face but not the terrified look I had seen so often under similar circumstances.

As I began my formal announcement, however, her reaction quickly turned to horror and she collapsed to the porch floor sobbing hysterically. With some effort, I did manage to get her into her home and seated although I failed miserably in calming her down. Fortunately, her next-door neighbor, a very pleasant woman about her age, heard her cries and came rushing over to help. I stayed with them for another hour or so and left only after giving both of them a timeline of what to expect going forward.

As I left her home, I was somewhat surprised by the large number of people standing quietly in her small front yard. Obviously, they had heard her screams and were standing by to offer assistance, presumably once the Army car pulled away. They politely stepped aside as I passed by, but I did notice one unusual thing out of the corner of my eye: a young man running full-speed straight toward the soldier's home. My assumption was that he had just heard the news and was going there to offer condolences to the family. Unfortunately, he had misread everything, turned toward me, and shot me in the lower back with some type of pellet gun. I fell to the ground amid cries and screams from the crowd, momentarily stunned. Clark, waiting for me by the car, ran to me, threw me over his shoulders, and tossed me into the back seat. Pretty amazing stuff since Clark was well up in his sixties and could not have weighed more than 140 pounds while I tipped the scales at over 200 pounds. Within fifteen minutes, we were in the emergency room of the Charleston Naval Base Hospital where my superficial wound was cleaned and bandaged.

Later that night, I received a telephone call and then a follow-up visit from the Charleston Police Department asking me detailed questions about the incident, apparently reported to them by the Naval Hospital. I explained why I was in that neighborhood that late at night and indicated that I was fully aware of the risks involved. I also made the case for the young kid who had attacked me, stressing that I was sure he had simply misread everything and was just trying to protect his neighbor. Eventually, they agreed to recommend that his fate be assigned to a Military Police unit, which I suspected would be much more lenient toward him once they had received my full report.

On my follow-up visit to the soldier's family the next day, the young man, escorted by his mom holding him by the scruff of the neck, raced over to apologize to me. Turned out that he was the soldier's best friend from childhood. I lectured him briefly, primarily for the benefit of his mother, suggesting that he learn to be a bit less impulsive. I then told them of the visit from the local police to my home the night before and the questioning that had taken place. They were not at all surprised to hear that bit of news; in fact, it was quite obvious that both expected it. They were; however, greatly relieved when I then told them that the local police would not be pursuing the matter further.

Interestingly, as we moved forward with the planning for the wake and memorial services, the young man proved to be an invaluable asset to the family, coming up with any number of suggestions that he knew his friend would have appreciated. He also gave a beautiful eulogy at the memorial service, vowing at the end to do everything possible to help his friend's family.

Unknown to me at the time, Colonel Campbell immediately explored the possibility of formally recommending me for the Purple Heart but was quickly rebuffed. Yes, the Pentagon agreed, I was wounded in the line of duty. No argument there; however, the incident did not occur in a combat zone. Technically true, but for anyone living in those times, an inner-city neighborhood, for a young white male, on a hot and humid late summer night, certainly bore some similarities to a combat zone. In its place, however, I was awarded the Army Commendation Medal which was created in 1945 for "Heroism, or Exceptional Meritorious Conduct in the Performance of Outstanding Services." The medal was presented to me by Colonel Campbell at a ceremony at the Depot on March the 3rd of 1967, my last full month of active duty. The accompanying citation highlighted my work with next-of-kin and family, stating in part that: "Lt. Motz' performance of duty in the sensitive areas of Casualty Notification and Survivors Assistance was particularly outstanding and he consistently displayed exceptional qualities of judgment, tact, and understanding in resolving the many problems with which he was confronted. His actions were designed to place consideration of the next-of-kin and family ahead of personal desires or convenience and in all cases, his performance was timely, effective, and designed in such a way as to increase public confidence in the Army." Quite an honor and a very nice cap to my active duty career.

CHAPTER 9

Related Assignments:
Special services officer for recreational activities; court-appointed best man at a soldier's quickie wedding; chairman of two boards investigating job-related civilian deaths; co-creator of a model Vietnamese village; evaluator of houses of prostitution.

As you can see by the above subtitle, I had a number of other responsibilities far removed from my work with bereaved families. None required much time away from that work and all were clearly of secondary importance. So, why even mention them? Isn't this a story about families in distress? A valid question and frankly one I never focused on until recently. The answer: I now realize that every one of those assignments played a critical role in enabling me to properly carry out my Casualty Notification & Survivors Assistance duties. What! How? Clearly, working with grief-stricken families was always my focus and my top priority – consoling them, reminiscing with them, taking them through the grieving process step-by-step, and assuring them that time would eventually help to heal their wounds. Not complicated, but both time consuming and stressful. Colonel Campbell, in his infinite wisdom, realized that and clearly felt that an occasional change of pace was important for my mental well-being.

He was right, of course, so I decided to include a chapter on some of those experiences. After all, a quickie wedding, a model Vietnamese village, and a legendary brothel – they certainly did help to refocus my mind to challenges of a different sort.

As the Special Services Officer, I was responsible for operating the Depot recreation facility, which included a 15 by 50 foot swimming pool, plus an indoor facility with vending machines, a changing room, bathroom and showers. It was located just behind the family quarters and was never crowded, except for peak hours of summer weekends, making it an ideal place for evening cookouts and a swim with my friends, both military and civilian. It was also a perfect fit with my earlier lifeguarding days in the Hamptons. The only challenge was keeping the pool water toxin-free, a difficult task thanks to the neighboring pulp and paper mill's frequent low-hanging clouds containing unhealthy levels of carbon monoxide, ammonia, chloroform, sulfur dioxide, and mercury.

Another special services assignment focused on coordinating the Unit Fund deep sea fishing outings for the officers assigned to the Depot. All but one of those semi-annual trips into the Atlantic were pure fun for everyone and great for morale. The one that wasn't, however, was pure hell. I was awakened on that fateful morning at 0500 by the sound of high winds and driving rain beating against my bedroom windows. Since the boat was scheduled to leave Charleston Harbor at 0700, I assumed that either my fellow officers or the captain of the boat would want no part of a fishing trip under those conditions. Wrong on both counts. A call to Colonel Campbell confirmed that, of course, the trip was on and a call to the boat captain failed to give me the excuse I needed to get it postponed.

So, we all gathered at the dock in downtown Charleston at 0630, dressed in our foul weather gear, boarded a substantial looking, albeit somewhat weather-beaten commercial fishing boat, and headed out to the Gulf Stream, 60 or so miles offshore, traveling at about 12-14 knots. As we cleared the harbor and hit the open water and the men got their first look at the size of the swells, several of them became suddenly in favor of heading back home and buying their catch at a local fish market.

The colonel would have none of it. *"Retreat is not an option!"* he bellowed.

We were in for the duration which meant a long day

on the high seas. This was *"an important character builder"* for all of us. In reality, long before we reached our destination, everyone on board was seasick save for the colonel and the captain. Unfortunately, not a single line was cast all day and, by the time the boat returned home early that evening, morale was….well…..poor. In hindsight, about the only benefit derived from the trip was a tighter bonding among the men unfortunate enough to have shared that experience on the high seas on a miserable day. Perhaps that was the colonel's objective, although I seriously doubt it.

A couple of other assignments led to some unusual and sometimes more challenging experiences. For example, I was called upon quite frequently to assist non-Depot active duty soldiers with legal issues created during furloughs in Charleston, almost always drunk and disorderly conduct or driving while intoxicated. In such cases, the solution was never that complicated, usually involving an early morning visit with the soldier at the jail to get his side of the story, followed by an appearance with him in court to plead his case, almost always in front of a judge sympathetic to the soldier's plight, and frequently ending with a stern lecture, warning, and/or a modest fine.

One case, however, was anything but ordinary. As the story developed, a 20-year old brand-new graduate of the Ft. Jackson basic training boot camp decided that the best way to mark his achievement was to celebrate his 72-hour furlough in Charleston, which he had heard was a lot more fun with prettier women than the area around Ft. Jackson. No argument there. He also had a car which he had driven down from his home in upstate New York, so why not?

Since he knew no one living anywhere near Charleston, he checked into an inexpensive motel just outside the city proper, got himself some food at a nearby Hardees Restaurant and headed off to the area surrounding the huge Charleston Naval Base complex which he had been told had the highest concentration of bars in the city.

He was relieved to see that just about everyone in those bars were dressed in their civvies which he felt would make it easier for him to fit in with what he assumed was primarily a Navy crowd. His first stop was a rather typical service bar located just outside the main gate of the base and it was crowded with a reasonably even mix of young men and women, most appearing to be about his age. One beer led to another and before long he was in a conversation with a half dozen men and women who seemed perfectly happy to welcome him into their group even after they discovered that he was not a Navy man. Neither were they. They were, in fact, all local residents doing exactly what he was doing: checking out a bar with an assumed heavy dose of Navy personnel.

As time passed, one of the women seemed to fancy him and she was cute with a good sense of humor. The evening was turning out even better than he had expected. Eventually, the group shrunk down to him and the cute girl. Clearly, they wanted to try something new, so they left the bar and piled into his car. Before long, he pulled over to the side of the road and climbed into the back seat with her.

After their fun, he offered to drive her home to North Charleston, an offer she was happy to accept since it was well past her midnight curfew. Thinking ahead to his remaining two days in Charleston, he asked for and received her phone number which motivated him to tell her his last name as well as the name of the motel where he was staying, just in case she wanted to pay him a visit. He was smitten!

Fast forward to approximately 0430 hours. I am awakened from a sound sleep by the ring of my telephone. No, it's not the Presidio with a death notification. It's a call from the desk sergeant at the Charleston County Jail, asking if I am still the go-to guy for Army issues in the

Charleston area. I reply in the affirmative.

His response: "We have arrested a soldier from Ft. Jackson on statutory rape charges and he wants to get some advice from an Army representative."

This was certainly a first for me, but it did fit into my job description, so I quickly dressed and headed off to the jail, located about 6-7 miles away. The facility was not a pretty sight. Not as bad as the old jail downtown on Magazine Street, now a tourist destination, but still not a pretty sight in the pre-dawn hours.

I arrived at sunrise and, after providing identification to the desk sergeant, was shown into a small interrogation room to meet the soldier, who was soon brought in, handcuffed and looking more than a bit hung over and terrified. He certainly understood that he was in trouble but didn't know why. Well, of course, the answer to that was simple: she was much younger than he imagined, just 15 years old, one year below the age of consent in the state, therefore the statutory rape charge.

As I was gathering some basic information from him, I heard a loud commotion in the hallway, immediately followed by a man bursting into the room and identifying himself as the girl's father. How he had managed to get that deep into the police station puzzled me for a moment until I noticed that he was on a first name basis with many of the senior guards.

After glaring at the soldier, he turned to me asking, "So, what are we going to do about this?"

A long discussion followed with my sole goal to find a practical solution on a rational basis. What that was, I had no idea, at least until I realized that the father's main concern was that his daughter might be pregnant.

That gave me a possible opening. "Let's check out that possibility before any irrational decisions are made."

His problem: he believed – motioning with his hands – that pregnancy couldn't be known "until you see the big belly." Nothing I said to counter that belief could convince him otherwise.

After an hour or so of making no progress, a possible solution came from a most unlikely source: the father.

"If he agrees to marry my daughter, I will persuade the authorities to drop the charges." When faced with the likelihood of a long prison sentence as the alternative, the soldier readily agreed to accept the marriage option. Now, if she agreed, we had a possible solution in hand. Unknown to me, she was waiting for her father at the front desk, so he left to speak with her. While he was gone, I asked the soldier if he was absolutely certain that he was ready to take the plunge and he assured me that he was, that his mom and dad married as teenagers and were still together. Shortly thereafter, the father reappeared with his daughter in tow.

The soldier proposed, on bended knee no less, and she accepted with the comment, "I always wanted to be married before I turned 18!"

Different strokes for different folks.

Problem solved and the deal set. All charges would be dropped but not until they exchanged vows which they scheduled for three weeks down the road. In spite of the circumstances, the bride-to-be made it abundantly clear that she wanted a "real wedding" with a wedding gown, bridesmaids, ushers, and a reception after the church service. Until that time, he would remain in prison, to be released into my custody on the morning of the big day, dressed in a tuxedo at the jail and then handcuffed to me until the "I do's" were exchanged.

When the big day arrived, I picked up the groom, and we headed off in my Corvette, top down on a surprisingly warm mid-winter morning. Quite a sight, I imagine, for anyone in a passing truck or bus seeing the passenger in a tuxedo handcuffed to me in my Army Dress

Blues. Not to mention that it made working the stick shift a bit of a challenge.

The wedding was perfectly planned and executed by the bride's family. At the appointed hour, the soldier and I, now officially his "best man," walked from the sacristy across the front of the church, still handcuffed together, and waited as the bride walked up the center aisle in front of her family and invited guests, escorted by her father and preceded by several bridesmaids and ushers. Judging by the excited squeals coming from the church pews, I assumed that many of those guests were her high school classmates. She looked extremely happy and not at all concerned about the big step she was taking. The ceremony was brief, the vows spoken, and as I leaned in to give the bride a congratulatory kiss, I discretely removed the handcuffs and wished them both a happy life together.

In spite of the rough start, this story did have a positive ending. She was pregnant, and she delivered a healthy baby boy just before I completed my Charleston posting. Several years later, during a visit to my extended family in Charleston, I located them and was pleased to see that they were still happily married.

Another unusual assignment awaited me in the early summer of 1966. I had just returned from a three-day furlough in New York to learn that William Campbell, a civilian laborer working down on our docks, had fallen off the side of a 110-foot tugboat that he was repairing and drowned. Under Army regulations, the death had to be investigated and, though technically not a Military Personnel responsibility, Colonel Campbell asked me to conduct the formal hearing surrounding the incident. My first order of business was to report my assignment to the case to the JAG (Judge Advocate General) office at the Army Materiel Command headquarters in Washington and to ask for their guidance in developing a proper protocol for conducting the hearing.

Once I felt a reasonable degree of comfort in moving forward, I convened the hearing and began taking testimony from the men who had witnessed the accident. This led to two immediate problems: none of the four eyewitnesses spoke much English – Gullah/Geechee being their primary language, and to further complicate things, they all had a different take on the sequence of events that led to the death. Fortunately, I had been made aware of the language problem beforehand and had hired an interpreter to help us over the rough spots. The problem was that the closer the witnesses came to the critical moment in their testimony, the actual fall, the faster they spoke, frequently switching mid-sentence from barely passable English to Gullah and then back to English, making for a serious challenge, even for the translator. Thankfully, the proceedings were being recorded so, when necessary, I would simply call a recess and the interpreter would listen to a replay.

One major positive: all four witnesses agreed on the most critical point: the man had a well-known and overwhelming fear of the water and when he went down, they all testified, he never resurfaced. Apparently, it was also well-known by his fellow workers that he tried, whenever possible, to work only on boats in dry-dock. That testimony, which was corroborated by his wife, made it quite easy to understand the conclusion reached by the coroner in his autopsy report: that the fall had triggered a massive heart attack, most likely killing Mr. Campbell before he even hit the water.

I received a far more enjoyable assignment in the spring of 1966. Colonel Campbell wanted to put on a show for Armed Forces Day that would finally compete with the shows traditionally put on by the huge Naval and Air Force bases. It was a tall order for sure. After all, the Naval Base had a selection of submarines, battleships, destroyers, and perhaps an aircraft carrier or two available for tours as well as regular visits from the famed Blue Angels aerobatic team. Not to be outdone, the Air Force Base offered a close-up look at their brand new F-14 fighter jet, tours of a huge C-5A transport plane, and frequent visits by their own aerobatic team, the Thunderbirds.

Our collection of old World War II landing craft and an aging rail fleet were lame crowd-pleasers by comparison. Yes, we did offer a short cruise aboard an LCU landing craft and a ride around the Depot in a rail flatcar, but clearly something else was needed to attract the crowds. Fortunately, we had an ace in the hole, a master sergeant on temporary duty at the Depot, who had just returned from a tour of duty in Vietnam. I had listened to his stories about the Army's contribution to the war effort and realized that our Armed Forces Day tribute should focus on that effort and our master sergeant on loan was the perfect person to turn that dream into reality.

Yes, he was the real deal, a one-of-a-kind character by any measure and a true-blue Army guy who loved the challenge the colonel proposed to him: "We need you to construct a 100% authentic Vietnamese Village here at the Depot. It must be first class and believable on every level and it must draw crowds from the Naval and Air Force Bases."

That challenge made, the good sergeant went to work, first selecting an isolated and somewhat swampy location at the Depot where he created an amazing replica of a small village by the Mekong Delta where he had most recently been posted. The completed village had three adobe homes with thatched roofs, an animal pen with live animals, a blacksmith shop, and a shrine, all surrounded by a moat with punji stakes, a draw-bridge over the moat, and a watch tower to guard against enemy intruders. In addition, for Armed Forces Day, two Vietnamese Army officers and a Vietnamese family, mother, father, and their two young children, who were living at Ft. Bragg, were brought on board to add to the authenticity of the village. The sergeant completed the project in less than a month, all the time working with his pet rock python snake draped around his neck.

Not surprisingly, our Armed Forces Day celebration was a huge success. In addition to the village, we also invited a detachment from the Third Special Forces Group (Airborne) out of Ft. Bragg to demonstrate hand-to-hand combat techniques as well as protocol for identifying and eliminating suspected enemy soldiers hiding out within the village. The crowds, spurred on by advance advertising in the local media, were enormous, the TV crews from the local stations carried the story on their evening news, the sergeant and his snake were a huge hit among all age groups, and I was sought out for autographs for the first and only time in my life by bunches of kids as I wandered around the village in my combat gear.

In another effort to put a little variety into my workday and perhaps to lighten the stress factor a bit, Colonel Campbell appointed me the Army representative to the Armed Forces Disciplinary Control Board for the southern quadrant of South Carolina. Thanks to the efforts of local Congressman L. Mendel Rivers, the chairman of the powerful House Armed Services Committee, all five branches of the military were well-represented in the area, Army, Navy, Air Force, Marines, and Coast Guard, and, as could be expected, a number of questionable businesses existed in that environment that needed to be monitored and evaluated for the health and safety of the men in uniform. Meetings were held every other month alternating between the Naval Base Officers Club and the Air Force Base Officers Club.

At my first meeting, held at the Air Force Base Officers Club, I couldn't help but notice that I was the junior officer on the Board by two or three grades. The express purpose of the meetings was twofold: to review and report on all inspections of off-limits establishments made during the prior period, and to assign reviews for the upcoming period. A number of the off-limit establishments were described as rundown bars, some dealing pot and cocaine on the side; however, the majority of the long-term violators were low-end houses of prostitution, really, really low-end, I would soon discover. Our job was to visit those sites unannounced, to determine if they had cleaned up their act sufficiently to warrant removal from the restricted list, a relatively rare occurrence, I was told.

The Board, either on its own or at the request of Colonel Campbell, handed me a rather interesting initial assignment: to pay a visit to the legendary Sunset Lodge in Georgetown, South Carolina, arguably the best known "House of Ill Repute" on the entire East Coast. Had they perhaps cleaned up their act enough to warrant removal from the restricted list? That hardly seemed likely, nevertheless, they were due for their semi-annual review. An interesting assignment indeed for the novice member of the Board.

Although I had driven past the Sunset Lodge on numerous occasions on the way to or from a memorial service in the area, I had never seen it up close. Located a couple miles south of downtown Georgetown on the west side of U.S Highway 17, the main north/south route to Florida before the advent of the Interstate highway system, it sat back from the highway, discretely hidden by tall evergreen trees. It was one of the more substantial homes in the area; a country home with awnings shading its windows.

The drive to the lodge several days later was peaceful and pleasant with none of the pressures I typically experienced when out on call to a family. And let's be honest, I was curious as to how I would be received by management and intrigued by the opportunity to immerse myself, professionally of course, into a very unfamiliar environment. Who wouldn't be? In hindsight, it would also prove to be the change of pace I probably needed more than I realized at that time.

I arrived on site in about an hour's time, just after 1300, and drove to the parking area which I noticed was discreetly located behind the main building and away from any prying eyes on Highway 17. It was a gorgeous day, not too hot or humid with a gentle breeze. The path to the door was pleasantly landscaped...a small manicured lawn, colorful and aromatic flower beds, and decorative hedges lining the way.

My knock at the door brought an immediate response in the person of an extremely attractive, young woman, dressed rather conservatively in a nice summer outfit. She welcomed me, took my hand, and led me into the parlor, which was decorated in a very warm and comfortable way, not at all ostentatious. After offering me a glass of champagne and exchanging some basic pleasantries, she asked me if she could "be of any service" to me. Certainly an interesting choice of words.

When I explained the official nature of my visit, she reacted very calmly, simply saying, "I'll tell Madam Hazel that you are here."

Several minutes later, I was escorted into the inner sanctum, a nicely decorated office, understated with original artwork by local artists, reflecting the outdoor beauty of the Lowcountry.

I'm not sure what I expected the woman who had run the Sunset Lodge for several decades to be like: soft and sweet or hard as nails. She was neither. Her demeanor was thoroughly professional, pleasant, but all business. She was reasonably attractive, appearing to be somewhere in her late fifties, clearly not speaking with an original Southern drawl, and seemingly delighted to see me. After greeting me with what seemed genuine enthusiasm, she immediately turned her focus to the steps that she had always taken to assure that her home was properly run.

"We have only the sweetest and most attractive girls of a certain age. All are intelligent and carefully trained with a strong focus on proper manners and etiquette. We also encourage them to stay on top of current events, both local and national, since all of the men they will meet are well educated and successful in their chosen careers. Your role, we instruct them, is to make their visit enjoyable and stress-free."

She also spent a considerable amount of time focused on the importance of proper hygiene and health. "Did you know that I have a full-time medical doctor on call to test the girls on an ongoing basis? If one of our girls develops a health issue, we take her off-duty until her health issue is cleared up and approved by our medical people. Their health and the well-being of our clients," she assured me, "are what matter most to me and are the keys to success in this line of work."

That said, she then buzzed in another extremely attractive brunette whom she introduced to me as Debbie from Georgia who had just arrived that week, asking me with a wink, "Would you like Debbie to give you a taste of our Southern hospitality?"

Tempting, oh yes, but I politely declined the offer. At that point, I told her that although she did seem to run a very strict operation, it would nevertheless have to remain off-limits to the military at least for the foreseeable future. Her reaction was not what I expected and it floored me.

"*Thank God*! I can't tell you how relieved I am to hear you say that. The last thing I need is to have the restriction lifted and be overwhelmed by hordes of military personnel." Interesting perspective and one that certainly caught me by surprise.

I thanked her for her time and headed for the front door which swung open just as I reached for the door handle. Standing in front of me, being royally greeted by all the girls, was a very well-known state politician, clearly no stranger to the ladies. At that moment, it all made perfect sense. The continued existence of the Sunset Lodge, which was clearly and blatantly operating outside the law for almost 30 years, owed its survival to two time-honored realities: it was a successful, non-cyclical business that generated significant cash plus a steady flow of tourists into the local economy AND, of equal importance, it was protected by the influential customers it serviced – judges, attorneys, politicians, and the like throughout the state, who were always treated royally by Madam Hazel and her girls.

Oddly enough, I had another encounter with that politician several weeks later at a ceremony honoring members of a South Carolina National Guard unit which had just completed a short-term voluntary tour of duty in Vietnam.

"Those are some mighty fine looking young women, right son?" Obviously, as a seasoned politician, he remembered our brief encounter at the Sunset Lodge.

As a footnote: when I reported back to the Board at the follow-up meeting a month or so later, I learned that each of the Board members in turn had been given the Sunset Lodge assignment as their baptism of fire with the logic being that if you could resist that temptation, you certainly would not be tempted by any of the other decidedly less compelling establishments on the off-limits list.

The Main Gate: Charleston Army Depot, South Carolina-1966.
(shot taken from the base H-13 helicopter)

US Army LCMs (Landing Craft, Mechanized) were a big
part of   the Depot's operations and inventory. They were
typically stored as above.

On April 7, 1964, ex-*USS Albemarle*, a WW II seaplane tender, emerged from moth balls. She was converted to an Aircraft Repair Ship, Helicopter, at Charleston, South Carolina. Conversion included a 50 by 150 foot helicopter pad mounted aft. Helicopters forwarded to the repair ship by barge were hoisted aboard by a pair of cranes, each boasting a lift capacity of 20 tons. On March 27, 1965, she was reclassified and renamed, and the USNS Corpus Christi Bay (T-ARVH-1) was assigned to the Military Sealift Command in Jan. 1966.

Depot Headquarters Building-1965.

The Depot pool--an important part of my "additional duties."

US Army H-13 helicopter--often used in remote notifications.

The Depot built and maintained a mock Viet Cong village for purposes
of counter-insurgency training.

Entrance to the Vietnamese "village"
across a moat filled with punji stakes.

109

The Vietnamese village was often staffed by ARVN soldiers and was
open for tours and displays.

A thatched mud hut within the village.

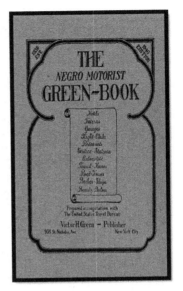

Mother Emanuel Church
downtown Charleston, SC.

An actual "Green Book."

A powerful visitor: a USAF "Phantom" 4-D fighter jet from the 555th
Tactical Fighter Wing. The "Phantom" was the workhorse fighter
aircraft of the Vietnam War, used by the USAF, the US Navy, and the
US Marine Corps.

"Zero Defects Day" Celebration at the Depot.

The US Army "Golden Knights" parachute team perform on "Zero Defects Day."

The Depot military bowling team.

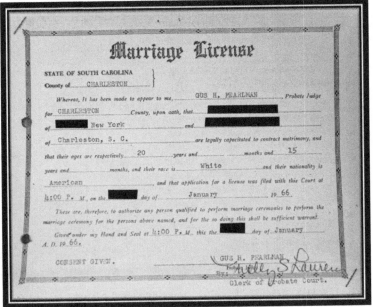

The "quickie wedding" marriage license.

The famous music box beer stein
from the "transfer of affections" case,

...and the "infamous" Sunset Lodge bordello, Georgetown, SC.

My prized 1966 Corvette "Stingray" convertible.

My first date with Mary: soon to be my wife and mother of our four
children.

My father enjoys a game of golf with Babe Ruth--early 1930s.

My young son, George, about to enjoy a ride on a huge LARC-5 on a
sentimental return visit to the Depot--early 1970s.

It is often said that a picture is worth a thousand words. Although I sincerely hope that I have been at least somewhat successful in conveying the depth of suffering, anxiety, and hopelessness felt by all families who experienced the loss of a loved one in the Vietnam War, I fully recognize the validity of that popular idiom.

CPL Harold T. Edmondson, Jr. an infantryman assigned to the 101st Airborne Division, was killed instantly by enemy small arms fire on January the 30th of 1966 in Phu Yen Province, South Vietnam. He was just nineteen years old. CPL Edmondson's case preceded the introduction of in-person death notifications by a member of the military, and was therefore not directly assigned to me. Nevertheless, these photos bring back a flood of memories – the church and cemetery for sure, a typical setting for a number of my memorial services and burials, but even more so, the look of utter devastation in the eyes of family and friends.

Funeral Services

for the Late

Harold T. Edmondson, Jr.

— AT —

EBENEZER A.M.E. CHURCH

44 NASSAU STREET
CHARLESTON, SOUTH CAROLINA
Dr. B. J. FINKLEA, *Pastor*

MONDAY, FEBRUARY 14, 1966

AT 2:00 O'CLOCK P.M.

•

— *Interment* —
ZION A.M.E. CEMETERY
12-Mile, Mt. Pleasant, South Carolina

Wainwright Printers

The photos on the following pages © Costa Manos/Magnum Photos

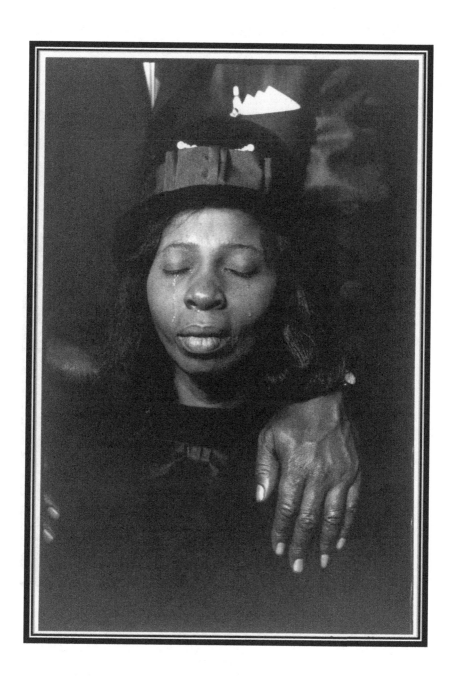

First Lieutenant George M. Motz, US Army-1966

CHAPTER 10

The Problems of a Home Wake:
A surprisingly challenging Survivors Assistance case.

Back now to the central theme of the book. We have seen that things did not always turn out exactly as planned while working a Casualty Notification or Survivors Assistance case. Thankfully though, problems were rare, and when they did occur, they were almost always resolved by those in charge with a bit of quick thinking and common sense. Most of the time, but not always. Let's take a look in this chapter and the next, at those exceptions. First, we will examine a Survivors Assistance case made challenging by an ill-advised decision by the family to have a two-day wake at their home. In the next chapter, we will analyze a Casualty Notification case on life-support thanks to a badly botched notification. Both required extensive damage control in order to assure a proper outcome for family and friends.

To my surprise, all of my early active duty Casualty Notification/Survivors Assistance cases involved black soldiers killed in action. Why only black soldiers? Although I have no definitive answer to that question, one strong possibility exists: many young black men from the area chose to enlist in the Army, perhaps seeing it as the best opportunity to improve their lot in life. As a result, my first case involving a white soldier was not assigned to me until mid-autumn of 1966. On the surface, it appeared to be a straightforward case. It was not. The soldier's family lived in a middle-class white neighborhood within the Charleston city limits, just a couple hundred yards south of the North Charleston line. It was an attractive neighborhood populated by 1950s era ranch-style homes, situated on small parcels of land, nicely landscaped, mixed in with some well-maintained, middle-income garden apartments.

I arrived at the home in the early evening, roughly two hours after receiving my instructions from the Presidio. My hope was that since it was after normal working hours, both parents would be there to help each other deal with the tragic news. My knock at the front door was quickly answered by the soldier's father who took one look at my solemn expression and immediately understood that I wasn't there to bring his family any good news. He called to his wife, who, based on the wonderful aroma coming from the kitchen, was preparing dinner for the family.

To me he simply said, "It's about Jimmy and it's not good, right? Has he been hurt badly?"

I confirmed that it was not good news and, as his wife approached, I added that Jimmy had been ambushed and killed while on night patrol. Shell-shocked and clinging to each other, they invited me into their home, clearly very anxious to learn more about his death as well as what they would need to do going forward. I filled them in on the few details at my disposal, assured them that I would be visiting with them daily, and gave them the timeline to focus on while awaiting the return of their son.

An hour or so later, as I was walking to my car, I was surprised to hear the father frantically calling after me, "**STOP!** I need to talk to you!" Thinking that perhaps his wife had fainted, I turned and asked him what was wrong. His response surprised me. "Did the Army have any life insurance on my son?" Thinking that I had misheard him, I asked him to repeat the question, which he did. In hindsight, my response was probably a bit insensitive considering his emotional state. "Let's go over that stuff after the memorial service." Undeterred, he continued, "Just give me an idea of how much life insurance my boy carried," to which I answered, "All servicemen and women serving in Vietnam are typically covered by a standard $10,000 life insurance policy."

That answer seemed to satisfy him although he did say as I got into my car, "Please don't tell my wife that I asked about that."

That exchange began a series of misadventures with that family that made the three-week experience quite memorable.

As promised, I returned to their home the following evening with the objective of laying out, in a general sense at least, what they needed to focus on in preparation for the return of their son. I had barely taken a seat at their dining room table when they hit me with a laundry list of requests.

"We would like to have a two-day wake,"-certainly a normal request- "with full military honors." No problem there. Happy to oblige.

Then came the surprise. "We would like the wake to be at our home."

Perhaps not an outlandish request on the surface, but a new one for me. One potential problem I immediately anticipated: the home, while attractive, didn't seem spacious enough to accommodate what I anticipated would be a large number of mourners. Not only was the combined living room/dining room very small, the dining area had an oversized table, a china cabinet and two sideboards. Another possible problem: there were two pre-teenage children living there. How would they react to having their brother laid-out quite possibly in an open casket in their living room? It was not my decision to make but one which needed to be discussed with the funeral director whom I immediately brought into the conversation. He also thought a home wake was a bad idea, stressing to the parents that the funeral home was far better suited to handle any surprises that might arise, sort of a "leave the worry to us" approach. Very wise advice in hindsight! The parents minds were made up, however, and not about to be swayed by our logic, so a home wake it would be. At that point in time, neither the funeral director nor I could possibly have imagined the challenges that decision would create.

On the first day of the wake, I drove over to the family's home late in the afternoon, arriving just as the men from the funeral home were putting the finishing touches on their work. The open casket certainly dominated the entire far left side of the living room, no question about that, but it was nicely offset by several impressive floral arrangements. Surprisingly, everything seemed in order. Yes, it was going to be a tight fit once the crowd arrived but perhaps the weather would remain pleasant, allowing the overflow to spread out onto the back lawn. Maybe I was just being too pessimistic. With that thought in mind, I drove over to the Charleston Naval Base Officer's Club for an early dinner with a goal of returning just prior to the start of the wake, scheduled for 1900 hours. Boy, was I in for a surprise!

I arrived back at their home just before 1830 and, in hindsight, it was fortunate that I did. The first thing I noticed as I walked into the living room was the casket, now closed. Maybe, I thought, the parents had realized that an open casket would just be too difficult for the young brother and sister to handle. Good for them. A very smart decision on their part. My relief was very short-lived; however, as I looked to the right and was blown away by a very disturbing sight, a sight that has stayed with me to this day. The soldier had been taken out of the casket and placed on the couch, legs up, left arm draped over the back of the couch. Could anything possibly have been more ghoulish than that? Actually, yes, mom snapping Polaroid pictures of her young children taking turns sitting in their brother's lap.

The soldier's father, seeing the shocked look on my face took me aside and explained that his wife was terribly distressed to see her son in a casket and begged him to help her move him to the couch, his favorite place to watch television. He realized that it was not a normal thing to do, but he was relieved to see that it did seem to calm her down a bit. He did admit; however, that the sight of her taking pictures of the kids sitting in their son's lap was over the top, and he was also nervous as to how the people coming to pay their respects would react to his son posed on the couch.

Fortunately, the mourners had not yet arrived, so I locked the front door, called the funeral director and requested some immediate help which was quickly provided but not before a few "I told you so's" on his part. Not surprisingly, the parents were not happy with my decision as well as with the delayed start, but I knew in my heart that the scene would be too difficult for many to handle. Once the soldier had been placed back in the casket, I unlocked the door and the wake officially began roughly 45 minutes behind schedule. For the rest of the evening, I kept a close watch on the mother and the soldier.

You might have thought, as did I, that mom would have understood that her son's body should not be tampered with after the day-one dramatics. Unfortunately, we would have been wrong to assume that. On the second day of the wake, I again arrived thirty or so minutes ahead of the viewing and immediately noticed a problem. No, thank God, his body was still in the casket; however, his forehead had turned a ghastly shade of bright purple. Why, I had no idea, but when I asked mom, she had a simple explanation. "My son's hair was parted on the wrong side, not the way he liked it, so I re-combed it and then, to make sure that it stayed in place, I sprayed it with my hair spray." Obviously, the hair spray had not reacted well with the chemicals the funeral home had used in the embalming process. This, of course, mandated another call to the funeral home, another series of "mea culpas" from me, and a visit by their cosmetician to restore the soldier's face to its natural color.

As you can well imagine, with that series of wake-related mishaps, I hated to think of what could or would go wrong at the memorial service and burial the following day. Thankfully, nothing went wrong. Quite the contrary: the memorial service was beautiful, the pastor, who obviously knew the family very well, gave a powerful eulogy, the church choir was in rare form, and the burial service at a small cemetery, a short distance from the church, went smoothly, thanks to a perfect performance from the Ft. Jackson Honor Guard Unit.

As a postscript, I completed my work on the case over the next couple of weeks, wrapping it up with an awards ceremony at the Depot, after which I handed the $10,000 life insurance check to the soldier's mother.

CHAPTER 11

A Captain's Folly:
A casualty notification gone awry.

The vast majority of my Survivors Assistance cases were completed, start to finish, problem-free. What's more, even when a seemingly significant problem surfaced, there was always enough time to resolve it to everyone's satisfaction. Of course, I also learned through experience to avoid obvious pitfalls early-on in the planning process – a home wake, for example. In a Casualty Notification, however, you had but one opportunity to get it right and, if you failed, the damage was devastating to the next-of-kin and family, and almost impossible to correct. This chapter examines the one notification that "got away" and the steps that were needed to minimize the damage, which both Colonel Campbell and I realized, had the potential to cast our efforts, as well as the new Army program itself, in a very negative light.

As highlighted throughout this story, very few of my Casualty Notifications were assigned to me during normal 0800 to 1600 office hours. Indeed, the vast majority of them came via calls to my home in the middle of the night. Other after-hour notifications, assuming I was unreachable, were fielded by the duty officer of the day and then passed on to me on a top priority basis.

That system worked flawlessly until one day when it did not. By the early summer of 1966, I was almost always working several cases simultaneously, all at different stages and spread out over an ever-expanding geographic area. In other words, I was a busy guy, a reality that my immediate supervisor, a long-term in-grade captain noticed and--unknown to me at the time--found disturbing, thinking that, because I was so busy, I was "becoming Colonel Campbell's fair-haired boy." His exact words expressed to several other officers at the Depot and, eventually, directly to me.

To digress for a moment, promotions in the military, whether on the enlisted or officer side, have always been the lifeblood of the system. In times past, at least on the officer side, one could fall into limbo, otherwise known as the less desirable "fully qualified not selected" category, forever. This rule was eventually changed in the late 1960s, I believe, to allow a limited number of such evaluations to be followed by either a mandatory retirement, if eligible, or a mandatory resignation. The change was put into effect in an effort to eliminate a systemic problem: mediocre talent blocking the promotion of well-deserving younger officers. The officer in this case received a field promotion to captain in early 1944, at the height of World War II, and had languished in that grade for some twenty years, having been repeatedly passed over for promotion. Did he deserve such treatment? I have absolutely no idea. However, to be honest, he was far from the fair-haired boy at the Depot, having made numerous blunders on special projects assigned to him by the colonel.

A case in point: he completely botched the biggest special assignment given to him, a project tailor-made to highlight an officer's organizational and leadership abilities. The assignment came about in the spring of 1966 and it was a big deal. We had been ordered by our headquarters, the Army Materiel Command, to establish a "Zero Defects" program at the Depot and, once implemented, to showcase it to the local community with an open-house spectacular. Logically, the captain's first order of business should have been a thorough review and analysis of the basic structures and operating principles of the three divisions at the Depot: Storage, Maintenance, and Administration, followed by specific guidance to senior management as to how and where improvements could be made. In other words, a top-to-bottom study with the sole focus on improving the overall operating efficiencies of the units responsible for executing the Depot's main mission. A tall order yes, but one which someone with his military background should have been able to handle without undue difficulty.

The captain accepted the challenge enthusiastically; however, rather than first stepping back and doing his homework on each division and only then proposing solutions to obvious problems, he launched an aggressive full-frontal attack with the predictable result: alienating virtually everyone with whom he had to work to reach his goal while simultaneously crushing morale with a high-handed attitude. As a result, by the time the deadline had arrived a couple of months later, overall operating efficiencies were below prior levels and the defects that had always existed in the system were not only still present but now magnified for all to see. Only a perfect "Zero Defects Day", the day set aside to celebrate the Depot's top-notch efficiency in front of many top federal and state politicians, the local news media, and the general public, could even begin to save the day.

The weather on the morning of Zero Defects Day was near perfect: bright and sunny, temperatures in the mid-seventies, and, as an added bonus, surprisingly low humidity, not at all a given in the Lowcountry at that time of year. Temporary seating had been moved into position along the edge of the Parade Ground, a printed schedule of events was handed to the guests as they arrived, and a soft drink stand stood ready to dispense free sodas and snacks to everyone. The crowds arrived early, and what a crowd it was – far more than had been expected. All in all, a promising start to the afternoon activities.

Colonel Campbell opened the ceremony promptly at 1300 hours, welcoming a large group of dignitaries including United States Senator Ernest Hollings,

Congressman L. Mendel Rivers, Rear Admiral Thomas Dorsey, Air Force Base Commander, Brigadier General William McBride, as well as over one hundred Charlestonians and most Depot employees, all looking forward to the festivities. He then turned the program over to the captain who launched into an unnecessarily long and tedious speech on the meaning of "Zero Defects" and the difficult challenges he faced in reaching for that goal.

Fortunately for all, his comments were followed by an outstanding opening act, the Army Golden Knights Skydiving Team, a relatively novel act some fifty years ago, which took center stage, executing a perfectly coordinated skydive from high above the Depot to a pinpoint landing on a bulls-eye target placed in the center of the Parade Ground. A great start to the festivities but unfortunately, the sole highlight of the afternoon. The first noticeable defect: losing the entire sound system shortly after the skydivers hit the ground, forcing the captain to use a bullhorn for the balance of the show. Was it sabotage by disgruntled employees upset by their treatment by the captain, or coincidence? Hard to say. In any event, one thing learned from the experience: bullhorns might be perfect for barking out orders at a chaotic scene, but not for speech-making. So much for zero defects and a successful afternoon.

The captain was also considered by his fellow officers to be a bit of an odd duck in certain aspects of his personal life. A visit to his Depot living quarters was enough to convince anyone of that. The quarters were standard Army officer's quarters, pleasant but modest, perhaps 1400 to 1500 square feet on one level, a typical 1950s ranch-style house. Plenty of space for an officer and a family of four or five and certainly more than enough space for the captain and his young wife, except for the fact that he had a rather unique take on home decorating. Seriously, what normal person would have more than a dozen enormous grandfather clocks in perfect operating order, wound and randomly set to different time zones and chiming virtually non-stop throughout the day and night?

With that as a backdrop, when a call came from the Presidio to headquarters just a couple of minutes after our 1600 hour closing time, it was answered by the Duty Officer who just happened to be the captain. Instead of reaching out to me, or placing a call to Mrs. Bercaw, which was the established SOP (Standard Operating Procedure), he saw the call as his opportunity to make the notification, thereby grabbing the spotlight for himself, an opportunity he certainly did not want to squander. His dilemma was not knowing if the Presidio would try to reach me at my home, thereby posing a threat to his perceived moment of glory. What to do?

Tragically, but perhaps not surprisingly, the captain made the wrong choice, and it would end up costing him dearly. Strict military protocol demanded a timely, *in-person*, notification, with no exceptions. The captain, fearing that he might miss out on this opportunity to shine in the colonel's eyes and unsure of how much time he had before the Presidio located me, decided to ignore protocol and place a telephone call directly to the next of kin, who happened to be a very young woman who had married the soldier just before he had shipped out to Vietnam. Once he had verified that he indeed had her on the phone, he blurted out, "Just in case you have not been contacted by anyone from the Charleston Army Depot, I want to be the first to tell you that your husband was killed in action in Vietnam," and then, unbelievably, he just hung up the phone.

Needless to say, all hell broke loose and in the end, it would prove to be a dark day, not only for the family of the soldier, but also for the captain. The young woman was living with her in-laws while her husband was overseas and her father-in-law witnessed the entire exchange and was livid. It would have been bad enough if he had been a civilian told of the death of his son in that manner and perhaps not realizing that it was a serious breach of protocol. But he was far from that. No, he was, in fact, the highest-ranking non-commissioned officer at the nearby Charleston Air Force Base. By the time I got wind of what had happened, he had reported the inexcusable lack of judgment and violation of protocol to Base Commander, Brigadier General McBride, who had immediately contacted Colonel Campbell in an absolute rage.

As all of this was taking place, I was quietly sitting at my small kitchen table in my off-post apartment ready to dig into a nice dinner of filet mignon, mashed potatoes, and creamed spinach, one of my favorite meals. Before I could take my first bite, however, my phone rang and as I picked up, all I could hear was Colonel Campbell yelling at me into the phone. "How in the world could you have done something so stupid? You've done enough of these notifications to know not to cut corners." Frankly, I had no idea what he was talking about. After what seemed like an eternity, I began to grasp the problem...a botched death notification, but I still had no idea what notification he was talking about since I had always followed strict protocol. He then gave me the name of the deceased soldier. Mystery solved: it was a new name to me. With that, he checked the Duty Officer log and saw that the captain was on call.

"Why am I not surprised?" he barked as he slammed down the phone to go after him.

After verifying that the captain had indeed made the notification, the colonel called me back and asked me to drive over to the sergeant's home to beg for forgiveness and understanding, assuring me that he would call the family immediately to offer his condolences and sincerest apologies.

Although I had handled numerous notifications by that time, this one promised to be among the most difficult, even though the actual notification had already been made.

The captain had assured that by his reckless actions. As I drove the short distance to the Air Base, I tried to anticipate the reception I would receive once I arrived at the sergeant's quarters. Clearly, he would be the focal point even though technically my first responsibility was to the next-of-kin, his daughter-in-law. I also would be going in blind, having no idea if Colonel Campbell had been successful in contacting him and, if so, how he had reacted to that call.

Any thoughts that I may have had of first talking to the next-of-kin were dashed as I pulled up in front of the home. The sergeant was standing outside on the top step of his front porch, arms folded across his chest looking downright menacing. My only positive take on that scene was that quite obviously, Colonel Campbell had spoken to him and told him that I was on my way over to talk to his family. The unknown, of course, was whether he had been able to convince him that the screw-up was not of my doing. As I walked toward his home, he came down the steps and met me mid-front-lawn, still with his arms folded across his chest. For the next 10-15 minutes, he proceeded to tell me exactly what he thought of the Army, all the while assuring me that nothing like that could ever, *ever* happen in the Air Force. Finally, by the grace of God, his wife came to the front door and persuaded her husband to invite me into their home.

Once inside, I was introduced to the young woman who was clearly shell-shocked and just in no condition to participate in the conversation, which by then was turning to the facts surrounding the soldier's death, as well as the projected schedule going forward. I filled them in on every detail at my disposal and promised I would pass along any and all additional information just as soon as it was given to me by my Army sources. I also explained, as I prepared to leave, that I would stop by daily to help them plan the memorial service and to guide them through any Army paperwork that needed to be processed. Being military people, they clearly understood the risks of their son's assignment to Vietnam and had prepared themselves as much as possible for such a loss although, of course, no one can ever be fully prepared for such news.

Arriving back home just before midnight, I placed a call to Colonel Campbell to give him a quick summary of my evening, promising a full report the following morning. My sense was that he was relieved to get my report although still furious at the mistakes that had mandated his "mea culpa" to the general and the sergeant.

Following a rather sleepless night, I dressed a bit earlier than normal, ate a light breakfast, and headed off to the Depot to complete my report to Colonel Campbell. As I approached the main entrance to the Headquarters Building just prior to 0700, I was surprised to see the captain standing by the front steps of the building, pacing back and forth. My gut reaction was that he was there to confront me on what had happened the night before. Why else would he be there that early? Did he know he had screwed-up big time or was he clueless and there to brag to me about his notification? I had absolutely no idea. The answer to that question soon became obvious, however, as I moved closer to him. Ashen-faced and seemingly very nervous, he approached me as I headed for the front door and told me that Colonel Campbell had called him at 0600 to tell him that he would be receiving orders at any moment to report to Ft. Riley, Kansas within 72 hours for further deployment "to a restricted area overseas." As we both knew, that was a sure sign that he was on his way straight to Vietnam since Ft. Riley was a key staging area for such deployments. Clearly, the colonel had wasted absolutely no time in meting out severe punishment for the captain's inexcusable lack of judgment and break with military protocol.

The memorial service was held three weeks later at the Air Base Chapel and it included an unusual combined

Army/Air Force presence, an Air Force chaplain and Army pall-bearers and bugler. All in all, it was a very well-planned, well-attended, and perfectly-executed send off for the young soldier. As a final note, the sergeant did come with his wife and daughter-in-law to the ceremony at the Depot honoring their son, during which Colonel Campbell presented the young widow with the Bronze Star and the Purple Heart which she, in a very emotional moment, handed to her father-in-law. At the conclusion of the ceremony, the sergeant took me aside to thank me for my help in assuring that his son received a proper farewell.

CHAPTER 12

Accidental Death, Murder, and Suicide:
The most difficult of all casualty notifications.

Yes, there were always aspects of every Casualty Notification that made them unique from the others, yet for me there was always the one constant: my apprehension preceding every single knock on a family's front door. Early on, I assumed that with time and experience, that part of the job would become at least somewhat routine. It never did. To this day, I can still recall each and every notification in vivid detail. In contrast, the important Survivors Assistance work had a much more positive feeling to it, simply because it allowed me to work closely with the family, to help them in a small way, as they prepared for the final tribute to their loved one, and after, as they began the long and difficult healing process.

Perhaps of no great surprise, the single most important factor determining the initial reaction of the next-of-kin to my arrival at their front door, was their perception of the degree of risk their loved one was facing in his assignment. Families of soldiers serving in Vietnam knew full well that his life was in danger day in and day out, thereby making my appearance less than a total surprise. Often though, especially in the earlier years of the war, I was greeted with a hopeful, "Oh, you must be the guy from my (son's, husband's, father's) unit. He said he would send someone over to say hello. How's he doing?" That, of course, added another dimension to my visit, especially when followed by my response: "No, unfortunately I never had the opportunity to meet him." Talk about an emotional rollercoaster for those poor people!

As the war expanded and the casualties mounted the mere appearance of my Army car at the curb, or of me in uniform walking up the front path, was often enough to cause the family of the soldier to come racing outside, their eyes filled with terror.

Non-Vietnam related deaths, a stateside automobile accident and a training related death, brought a completely different dynamic into play. In those two cases, the family was totally unprepared for my opening words:

"The President of the United States, the Department of the Army, and the People of the United States, regret to inform you that your son died as a result of: (an automobile accident/a training mishap). He died at approximately...."

Those deaths, perhaps understandably, led to an initial feeling of outrage against the Army for not protecting the loved one in its care. This was particularly true with a training death. As a result, my goal following that notification was to do my best, during the critically important post-notification days, to explain that, although the Army expended a great deal of time, effort, and expense to reduce all risk to a soldier, there were simply no guarantees that occasionally things would not end up very badly. The key was to help the family understand that the Army had indeed done its best to keep their loved one safe and out of harm's way.

Yet another dynamic came into play during a murder notification assigned to me toward the end of 1966. The initial report indicated that one soldier stood accused of causing the death of another in a late-night bar room fight in a neighboring state. In a murder case, you were required to pass that critical information on to the next-of-kin at notification and to inform them that the death would be fully investigated by a panel of officers with court martial authority and, that they would be encouraged to attend those proceedings, as well as an actual court martial, should probable cause mandate that one be empanelled.

From a totally practical standpoint, since the remains in this case were stateside, the timeframe between notification and the return of the body was considerably shorter. This proved to be a double-edged sword. On the one hand, it did force the next-of-kin and family to quickly focus on planning for the memorial services; however, on the other hand, it gave us less time to help them get over the initial shock and cope with the stark reality that confronted them.

In this particular case, it became quite obvious to me by a quick reading of the full Military Police report, which was not yet available to the family, that the soldier we were burying was almost certainly the primary cause of the fight that ended in his death. In other words, the report clearly stated that he was heavily intoxicated at the time and that he had, according to multiple witnesses, attempted unsuccessfully to lure a young woman at the bar away from her husband. A fight ensued and the husband eventually inflicted the fatal wound on the soldier.

As you can well imagine, even without that information, the wake and funeral were going to be very difficult. Had they been aware of that allegation, there was no telling how the soldier's wife or parents would have reacted, very possibly quite differently, considering the circumstances surrounding the death. Yes, they would most likely have to face that issue eventually, but it didn't seem appropriate for me to bring it up before the funeral.

Delivering an effective eulogy was always a challenge under the best of circumstances but in this case, it was nearly impossible. Nevertheless, a eulogy was an important part of the military tribute, expected by the next of kin, family, and friends. My approach was simple: I kept my comments brief and focused on the soldier, his accomplishments during his time in the military, with a special focus on several awards he had earned during basic training, reading the supporting citations word for word from the pulpit.

As difficult as combat-related, accidental, and murder notifications were, one other was in a league by itself – the suicide notification. Not only were you required to announce the death, you were also required under Army regulations to tell the next-of-kin right up front that, "...he died as a result of a self-inflicted wound", an absolutely horrible left-right punch to the already devastated family.

With that thought in mind, and in spite of having made many notifications, my drive to that soldier's home bearing that terrible news filled me with dread. Only 20 years old, he had completed basic training at Ft. Jackson and volunteered for an assignment to Vietnam. Unfortunately, from his perspective, he received a last-minute assignment to Korea, to the DMZ (Demilitarized Zone), the actively patrolled barren strip of land separating North Korea from South Korea. Tension at the DMZ was an on-going reality and it often led to widespread and recurring rumors of periodic skirmishes between the opposing forces. Our government vehemently denied those rumors, but they persisted nonetheless, and were given added credibility as soldiers returned from that posting with new stories of dangerous confrontations. My concern was not knowing if the family was aware of those rumors and, if so, whether they gave them any credibility. Also, on a more basic level, I did not know if they knew or suspected that he had any psychological issues before his overseas deployment. Too many unanswered questions.

One positive of sorts: the soldier's next-of-kin, his new bride, also 20 years old, was living with her husband's parents during his overseas assignment. Always good to have as many close relatives as possible present at that critical moment, although it certainly did very little to make this notification any easier. I was greeted at the door by the soldier's father who immediately invited me into his home. His wife and daughter-in-law were right behind him, sitting in the living room, both giving me a puzzled look. I soon saw fear in both parents' eyes although the young woman remained calm and seemingly just curious as to why in the world I was there.

After I told them the horrible news, the bride was speechless and the parents looked at me, first with a blank stare, then a look best described as bewilderment, followed by one of utter confusion, and finally, one of anger at the thought of suicide. Mom was the first to speak. "There is no way that our son would take his own life. He was brought up with good Christian values. It's all an ugly lie." An understandable reaction for sure but not an easy one to deal with.

I should mention here that as a result of those non-combat notifications, whether the cause of death was a training accident, suspected murder, or suicide, I did submit a proposed revision to the Army Manual which focused on a less rigid delivery, allowing for a proactive approach by the officer assigned to the case. In reality, keeping to the rigid announcement was next to impossible in those cases and, in any event, it lacked the sensitivity that such a delicate announcement demanded. It was my understanding that some of those suggestions did find their way into the manual after I completed my active duty obligation.

Several days after the notification, I had my first opportunity to meet one-on-one with the young widow who still found the thought of suicide impossible to accept. As we talked, however, it became increasingly apparent to me that she may well have triggered her husband's self-destruction, totally unintentionally. How could that be? Well, in our conversation, she explained that her husband's biggest concern as he prepared to head overseas was that she be comfortable and not spend all her waking hours worrying about him. She then shared with me copies of several letters she had recently sent to him in which she described in great detail all the fun things she was doing with their mutual friends, all designed to keep her from constantly worrying about him: movies, picnics, beach parties, concerts, and so on.

Then, quite possibly, the smoking gun. "You remember Bobby, my old boyfriend? Well, he has been really terrific, doing just one nice thing after another to keep me happy."

I could only imagine, a young kid, thousands of miles from home, in a frigid and isolated corner of the world, dealing with such news from home. Not my call, but it certainly seemed to be a possible motive for the soldier's actions.

Of course, such thoughts were pure conjecture on my part, so I kept them to myself. Better that his parents deal with the situation in their own way and in their own time, without adding a factor that could very easily have turned them against their daughter-in-law, with whom they seemed to have a very good relationship.

The planning for the memorial service was more difficult than most because the soldier's family found it so difficult to move past "the 800-pound gorilla in the room," the suicide--to focus on the decisions they needed to make. Fortunately, the funeral director and I had worked together on a number of other services and so we were able, thanks largely to his gentle prodding, to resolve all issues before the soldier was returned home.

On the day before the funeral, a last-minute announcement by the father threatened to change the dynamics of the send-off: he told his wife and daughter-in-law that he was going to speak out at the service to "debunk" the suicide theory. Clearly, he had every right to do so, assuming that his daughter-in-law didn't object; however, since no one outside of the immediate family had any clue that suicide was the presumptive cause of death, it seemed unwise, and certainly unnecessary, to bring it up in a eulogy.

This put the daughter-in-law in a quandary: she didn't want to upset her in-laws, but she also didn't want that issue addressed at the service. I suggested that she talk to her mother-in-law who seemed a bit more open-minded about accepting the possibility of her son's depression and perhaps a bit more openly protective of his legacy. They talked it through and agreed that it should not be mentioned at the memorial service; however, neither of them wanted to talk to the father about it, so they requested that I be the one to reason with him. It was not something I looked forward to but, under the circumstances, it was perhaps the only way of avoiding an embarrassing situation for the family.

My message to the father was simple and straightforward. If he decided to make his statement at the service, not only would it unnecessarily open up the likelihood of smearing his son's reputation among some narrow-minded folks within the community, it would also overshadow all the good things that his boy had done in his short life, which properly should be the only focus of the eulogy.

The response from the father was non-committal. Yes, he understood my reasoning and he would take it into consideration, but he would not commit to stepping aside until he evaluated the situation during the service. Although that was not what the two women had hoped to hear, it at least pointed to a possible break in his resolve.

The memorial service was quite exceptional and the pastor, in his moving eulogy, had nothing but positive reflections on the soldier and his service to his country. Then came the moment of truth. The pastor asked if anyone else would like to say a few words. The father looked over at me totally expressionless, rose from his seat, walked slowly up to the pulpit, took out some notes from his pocket, looked out at the assembled crowd, sighed, ... and introduced me as the Army representative who would talk to them about his son. As I began speaking, I made eye contact with the family sitting directly in front of me and saw total relief in the eyes of the two women closest to the soldier, thankful that the focus was going to be on nothing but positive aspects of his all-too-short life.

CHAPTER 13

Transfer of Affections:
A common psychological reaction to sudden loss of a loved
one.

"General Truman is holding on line one." With those seven words from Doris Bercaw came one of the most unusual challenges of my Army career. My reaction: why in the world would General Truman be calling me? Not only was Lt. General Louis W. Truman a three-star general and nephew of former President Harry S. Truman, he was, most importantly from my perspective, the Commanding General of the Third Army, a vast area covering the entire Southeastern quadrant of the United States. I simply couldn't imagine any scenario with a positive answer to that question. My first thought was, "What could I have done wrong?" Yes, the Charleston Army Depot was within the geographic territory of the Third Army; however, we were not part of the Third Army. We were, in fact, a support unit of the Army Materiel Command headquartered at the Pentagon. Nevertheless, General Truman was General Truman, so I assumed that whatever had led to his call was beyond important. So, nothing to do but take a deep breath, pick up the phone, and introduce myself.

His response, "Lieutenant, I have a serious problem here that I need to talk to you about." Certainly not the response I was hoping to hear, but hardly a surprising one. He continued, "There has been a major screw-up and from what I have been told, you are the best person to fix it."

Whew! With that, he brought me up to date on the problem. In short, a career army sergeant had been killed in action in Vietnam. His wife, a German citizen, had left Charleston and gone back to Germany to be with her family while her husband completed his overseas assignment. An army colonel had properly notified her in Germany of the death, and then delegated the follow-up of arranging her transportation back to her home in Charleston to a more junior officer, who booked her on a military flight for the following day to the Charleston Air Force Base. So far, so good. Unfortunately, someone failed to double-check their work and the widow was put on a flight not to Charleston but to McGuire Air Force Base in New Jersey, adjacent to the huge Ft. Dix Army Post.

When she landed at McGuire, confused, tired, and late at night, she had no option but to go on a military bus to the Reception Center at Ft. Dix in the company of a number of soldiers who had just returned from their year's tour of duty in Vietnam. Naturally, they were in a great mood and swapping war stories from the front lines, hardly something that the new widow needed to hear. Dropped off at the Reception Center, she was then told that there were no overnight accommodations available, forcing her to sleep on a couch at the center.

By morning, fit to be tied, she was put in touch with the Military Personnel Office at Ft. Dix which immediately made arrangements to fly her out of McGuire on the next available flight to Charleston. Unfortunately, once again, and you can't make this stuff up, the plane she was put on did not go to Charleston, but rather was re-routed at the last minute to the Pensacola Naval Air Station in Florida. It was at that moment that she quite justifiably lost her temper and placed a call directly to General Truman whom she knew commanded Third Army since her late husband had been stationed at the Army Infantry School at Ft. Benning, Georgia several years earlier.

Thus the direct order from General Truman: "Make this mess go away. Use whatever resources you need and keep me posted on your progress." Simple and straightforward.

My first step was a no-brainer: locate her and

arrange to get her on a plane to Charleston ASAP. A call to the Pensacola Naval Air Station confirmed that there was a plane scheduled to fly to Charleston that afternoon at 1400 hours. *Perfect!* I made a reservation for one under the name of General Truman. Next up, my first serious challenge: get her on the phone and convince her to board yet another military flight.

Fortunately, General Truman's aide had obtained the necessary contact information from her which he passed on to me adding that, "I don't think I have ever seen General Truman so furious." Not a good bit of news, but hardly surprising under the circumstances.

Apparently, according to the aide, the woman had all but threatened to take the whole incident to the press. Considering the amount of bad publicity the military establishment was already being hammered on a daily basis, this was one headline no one needed.

Using the information supplied to me by the major, I was able to contact the widow who was truly beyond outraged by her treatment since being notified of the death of her husband. So much so, in fact, that early on in the call, I was all but 100% certain that she was going to give me a piece of her mind and then just hang up, which would have put the mission in serious jeopardy and placed me in serious trouble. Fortunately, a bunch of mea culpas later, coupled with my bold-faced promises that no more mistakes would be made by the Army, finally brought her on board and willing to give the Army one last chance to do things right. I promised her that I would be on the tarmac when the plane landed in Charleston and then persuaded the major in Pensacola to escort her directly onto the plane.

I arrived at the Air Force Base close to an hour ahead of the scheduled landing with permission in hand to await her arrival just off the tarmac. Once the plane had landed and taxied up to a point maybe fifty yards from where I was standing, I braced myself for the inevitable confrontation that I was sure lay just ahead. As the passengers disembarked, I quickly saw that picking her out of the crowd was a piece of cake. She was the only woman on board. The expression on her face spoke volumes: she was livid! When I approached her and introduced myself, she chose to take that moment, right there on the tarmac, to relive the horror of her previous 36 hours in excruciating hour-by-hour detail, all thanks to the United States Army. This promised to be a major challenge and one that I simply had to win.

The first bit of information I learned was that her home in Charleston had been rented out during their absence, making finding a place for her to stay over the next several weeks priority number one. I drove her back to my office and, after a brief discussion, made a reservation for her at the classic Francis Marion Hotel in downtown Charleston. That seemed a logical choice since she had seen very little of the charm of the downtown area in the years since they had purchased their home in an outlying suburban community. I also thought it might be better for her to be in a quiet place away from the heavy military presence in North Charleston while she worked to regain her emotional strength.

We spent a couple of hours at the office preparing a rough timeline for the period just ahead, after which I drove her to the Francis Marion, checked her in, and invited her to join me for dinner in the main dining room. By the time we had finished our meal, prime ribs for both of us, a glass or two of red wine for her and a couple of glasses of iced tea for me, I suggested that we meet again the following afternoon to start planning for the memorial service. Although there was still a lot of work to be done, I did sense that she was beginning to relax just a bit which gave me hope that our mission had at least a modest chance of success, a feeling that I conveyed to Colonel Campbell and General Truman the following morning. I continued to meet with her on a daily basis and her mood continued to improve. The downtown accommodations combined with contacting family and friends and planning for the memorial service were helping to keep her focused and reasonably relaxed. Her daily strolls south of Broad Street to see the beautiful antebellum homes and gardens were also proving to be quite therapeutic.

Although in those days it typically took twenty-one days for a body from Vietnam to arrive at its final stateside destination, the sergeant's remains were shipped to Charleston in a record-setting sixteen days, most certainly thanks to a word or two from General Truman. Adding to that positive note, an inspection of the body at Stuhrs Funeral Home in downtown Charleston revealed that it was perfectly suitable for viewing by family and friends. This was especially important since, unlike many next of kin who appreciated me taking on the responsibility of advising them on an open or closed casket, I knew for sure that she would insist on a private viewing, even if the body was in very bad shape.

With the soldier back home, we set the date for the wake at Stuhrs, the memorial service at a Methodist Church in downtown Charleston, and the burial with full military honors at a cemetery just outside of Charleston. Since most of their close friends were military stationed around the world and since members of her family were unable to make the trip from Germany, the services were simple and attended mostly by his parents and their friends, many of whom were retired military living in the area. Everything went off without a hitch and the honor guard unit in particular did an outstanding job, perhaps spurred on by the fact that the soldier was a career Army man and a true hero, having been awarded a number of battlefield medals.

Several days after the services, with the paperwork completed, the time had arrived for the awards ceremony presided over by Colonel Campbell, followed by her return home to Germany to begin the healing process. Clearly, her family and friends were anxious to have her back with them and, from a practical standpoint, since her home in Charleston remained under lease for another six months, it seemed the logical thing to do. With a helpful call from Colonel Campbell to Brigadier General McBride at the Air Force Base, a reservation was made on a MATS (Military Air Transport Service) flight from Charleston to an eventual landing at Rhein-Main Air Base close to her family home in Frankfort. In addition, in view of the earlier issues in the case, the colonel was also able to land an invitation for lunch with General McBride at the Officer's Club. Clearly, this was above and beyond the call of duty and just as clearly, she recognized it as such and was very appreciative. The lunch itself was the perfect final step in the mission. The general was charming, the food excellent, and I had all the confidence in the world that this difficult challenge was drawing to a positive conclusion. All that remained was a short drive to the runway and my final farewell. Or so I thought.

When we arrived at the boarding site, I was told that the crew of the C-130 troop transport had been instructed to board her first. Another nice touch. Time for a final farewell.

As we were motioned forward, she turned to me and said, "I can't go back to Germany. I want to stay here with you."

Panic on my part. I knew in my heart that I had done absolutely nothing intentionally to encourage that feeling on her part. Frankly, romance was the farthest thing from my mind as I navigated through the treacherous waters of her emotions. Unfortunately, at that time, I had never heard of the psychological phenomenon commonly referred to as "transfer of affections". Going purely on instinct, I suggested that she was just overwrought by all that had happened in her life over the past month, and that once she was back home with family and friends, she would soon be ready to move on to the next chapter of her life. Thankfully, she did agree to board the plane and at approximately 1500 hours she was airborne and I was on my way to the Depot to file my final report and pass on the good news to both Colonel Campbell and General Truman. Unfortunately, that report, although accurate at that moment, did prove to be just a bit premature.

Apparently, the flight back to Germany and the reunion with family and friends failed to take her mind completely off her overall Charleston experience. Daily telephone calls to my office and home started the day after she arrived back home and continued day after day for a solid two weeks. The calls were brief, each averaging just a few minutes, and were always focused on things going on in Charleston. Pretty bland stuff and certainly nothing with any romantic edge. Then, just like that, they stopped, giving me hope that she had finally realized that her emotional state while in Charleston was playing tricks on her true feelings. Once again though, not quite the end of the story.

Several days after her last call, and just as I was finishing a quiet lunch at my desk, the serenity was suddenly shattered as she came charging into my office, a huge smile on her face, both hands thrust high in the air literally shouting, *"Surprise!"*

That it was. I can only imagine what my expression looked like and for Mrs. Bercaw, sitting just across from me, the look was priceless, capped by a very dramatic roll of her eyes.

As she sat talking to me, I noticed Colonel Campbell glance in my direction as he passed by my office and sure enough, several minutes later he called me on the phone with a simple question: "That's not who I think it is, is it?"

When I confirmed that it was indeed her, he ordered

me up to his office. As I walked in he looked at me and said, "So, you apparently are just too irresistible to stay away from. Wonderful!"

Clearly, his main concern was the possibility of a negative reaction from her should she feel rejected.

"Not to worry," I assured him. "Once she spends some time with me she will quickly realize that the flawless problem solver of her dreams bears absolutely no resemblance to the real me. Give it two weeks max."

In hindsight, I was flattering myself. Actually, it took her only three days to discover the real me, flaws and all, at which point she was more than happy to return to her family in Germany. Both Colonel Campbell and General Truman were decidedly relieved to receive my final report.

The rewards for my efforts included a very sweet letter from the widow packed inside a German music box beer stein, and very favorable letters of commendation, one from General Truman, the other from Colonel Campbell. In addition, the colonel threw in a 72-hour pass and a supersonic flight aboard an F-4 Phantom fighter jet from the Charleston Air Force Base to the Suffolk County Air Force Base on Eastern Long Island, enabling me to enjoy a full summer weekend of fun in the sun. The flying experience, covered in more detail a bit later, complete with a near vertical take-off followed by a spiral dive and a series of barrel rolls, was well beyond thrilling. Happy to have done it once but not something I would choose to do for a living.

There were several other cases which I guess could be loosely put into the "transfer of affections" category. Most were of very short duration, however, and strictly limited to the period between the initial notification and the final post-funeral wrap-up work. In hindsight, they were basically normal reactions from new widows shocked by their loss and subconsciously appreciative of anyone there to help them through their ordeal.

CHAPTER 13

One case; however, was not quite as simple, a notification to a 21-year-old woman who had married her high school sweetheart shortly after graduation, a rash decision in the eyes of her parents. His solution: enlist in the Army to prove his mettle. Following the standard basic training boot camp at Ft. Jackson, he was shipped overseas and assigned to a unit in Vietnam. Within just a few months, he was ambushed while on patrol and killed instantly.

On the surface, this notification did not appear to be particularly unusual except for one glaring fact that I noticed immediately but refused to believe: the young woman seemed considerably less traumatized by the tragic news than any other next-of-kin with whom I had worked. His parents, on the other hand, with whom she was living at the time, were quite naturally flat-out devastated. The contrast was so obvious to me that I found myself praying that mom and dad would not pick up on it which, as far as I could tell, they did not. In any event, I kept my primary focus on the next-of-kin but made sure to include the parents in all discussions. Fortunately in a sense, the widow was perfectly happy to have her in-laws make all key decisions on the wake and memorial service, which helped immeasurably to keep us on course during the wait for the return of the soldier.

Another oddity I thought, was that the majority of the mourners who came to the wake and funeral were friends of the parents with very few there to console the daughter-in-law, even though both she and her husband had spent their entire lives within walking distance of the church. Then, on the morning of the memorial service, as she and I were walking into that church, she turned to me and said, "I can't wait for this whole thing to be over with so I can get on with my life."

In the weeks that followed, I met with her in my office several times to wrap up the remaining paperwork and to set a date for the award ceremony. At the conclusion of that ceremony, which was attended by the young woman and the soldier's parents, I wished them well and closed the case. Not quite the end of the story.

Barely two weeks later, on a Saturday afternoon, I was home having a late lunch and watching a miniature golf tournament on television. Yes, as strange as that may sound, televised miniature golf tournaments were a popular attraction on summer weekend afternoons in the Southeast during the 1960s, with competition mainly between individuals or teams from the Carolinas and Georgia. My viewing was interrupted by a knock on my front door. No, I wasn't expecting anyone, but it was not unusual for a friend to stop by for an unannounced visit. When I opened the door, however, I found myself face to face with the young widow. Before I could say anything, she simply gave me a big smile and, without saying a word, opened her raincoat, the only article of clothing she had worn for the visit.

What to do? One option was to invite her into my home and attempt to explain "transfer of affections" to her in the privacy of my apartment. Certainly a logical approach to a delicate situation but one fraught with obvious risks, not to mention very serious temptation. After all, I was single and only a couple of years older, and she was very attractive. Or, I could just invite her in and throw caution to the wind. Tempting for sure, no denying that. Or, I could and did pick option number three: go outside with her, raincoat safely buttoned-up, sit on the front lawn, and calmly explain why she was acting that way and at least let her know that it wasn't a good way to start a relationship with anyone.

"Yes," I assured her, "you are extremely attractive," no lie there, "*but* you really need to slow down and take the time to figure out what you want out of life going forward."

She pouted a bit at the rejection but did eventually promise to go slow on future new relationships. We then

159

parted on good terms.

The following Monday morning, I walked into Colonel Campbell's office and told him what had happened. He slowly shook his head side to side and gave me a simple response, "You're a better man than I."

CHAPTER 14

Off Duty Fun and Games:
Judge at a beauty pageant; "hitchhiker" on a fighter jet;
"petrified passenger" aboard a pre-World War II plane;
"crew member" on a nuclear submarine; "navigator" on a
special helicopter flight; "kegler" on the threshold of
bowling immortality.

By this time, it should be pretty obvious to those of you following this storyline, that I had very little control over my daily schedule. First and foremost, I was on call 24/7 to respond to requests to make new casualty notifications, always my number one priority. In addition, thanks to my work on the Armed Forces Disciplinary Control Board, I was required to make random, unannounced off-hour inspections of sleazy bars selling the drug of your choice; and, with the exception of the Sunset Lodge, equally sleazy whore houses. In other words, I was not a 9 to 5 desk jockey. Far from it.

As a result of the unpredictable schedule, I almost always found myself squeezing in recreational activities during whatever free time I could scrounge up, often at the last minute. Perhaps not surprisingly, all of those activities were somehow related to my military service, but nonetheless, far removed from my day-to-day work. How, for example, could I turn down the opportunity to represent the Army at the Miss North Charleston beauty pageant? I couldn't, I didn't, and it was a hoot.

The request came from the North Charleston Chamber of Commerce in mid-1966. Their idea was to highlight to the community the positive aspects of the powerful military presence in their midst by selecting a young officer from each of the five branches of service to act as judges at their annual beauty pageant, the first step on the way to the Miss America crown. Probably because I was the youngest officer at the Depot and also single, or perhaps to give me a break from my stressful daily focus, Colonel Campbell selected me to represent the Army. I was more than happy to accept the assignment.

The contest was held poolside on a Saturday evening at a Community Recreation Center in the North area. It drew an impressive crowd of several hundred residents plus a couple dozen participants, all of whom were very attractive. Here was the eye-opener for me: seeing a beauty pageant from a totally different perspective. Simply put, under normal circumstances, I could easily imagine myself smiling or flirting with those young ladies as they paraded past in formal attire and bathing suits, but now the tables were turned. Yes, I became the stoic observer and the young ladies did the smiling and flirting in a not-too-subtle effort to sway our votes in their favor. It was a strange twist to be sure but certainly a most enjoyable one from my perspective.

Oddly enough, a number of my other off-duty experiences related to military air travel. I say oddly enough because I have never been a big fan of flying. From my very first plane trip in November of 1959 aboard an Eastern Airlines Propjet Electra from National Airport in Washington, D.C. to Idlewild Airport in New York, I have always boarded flights with a fatalistic, "Well, I have had a good life" mentality. Safely landing at the scheduled destination to this day has always been an unexpected bonus.

With that as a backdrop, I had several memorable flying experiences while on active duty. The first, and clearly the most thrilling, was the fighter jet flight from the Charleston Air Force Base to the Suffolk County Air Force Base on the East End of Long Island. The trip was arranged, unknown to me, by Colonel Campbell as a reward for some work I had done on the difficult "transfer of affections" Survivors Assistance case. All I knew on that beautiful mid-summer Friday afternoon was that I had been ordered to report to Brigadier General McBride's office at the Air Base at 1600 hours. I had absolutely no idea why.

When I arrived, I was quickly ushered into his office where he informed me that I had been given a 72-hour pass by Colonel Campbell and that to take full advantage of it, one of his men would fly me to New York aboard an F-4 Phantom fighter jet. This was the plane soon to be used by both the Navy Blue Angels and the Air Force Thunderbirds in their aerobatic shows. I was at once speechless, excited, and a bit petrified, not at all sure that I would literally be able to stomach the ride, but at the same time realizing that it was a once in a lifetime opportunity. Sensing my apprehension, he assured me that the pilot was a decorated veteran just back from Vietnam and one of the best pilots in his command. He then summoned the pilot and, following a brief meet and greet, we headed off to the plane which was waiting for us just off the runway on the Air Base side of the Charleston Airport complex.

As we walked to the plane, the pilot gave me a quick tutorial on procedures to be followed during the flight, highlighting the steps to be taken in the unlikely event of an airborne problem, not music to my ears, although his casual approach did go a long way toward eliminating most of my worries. Once seated, strapped into my seat, and hooked up to an oxygen mask and headset, the final systems checks were completed, and we taxied to our take-off spot. A few minutes later, we were on our way, roaring down the runway for what seemed like just a couple of seconds and then rocketing into the sky at what surely was close to a pure vertical climb. Nothing subtle about that takeoff! Shortly thereafter the plane leveled off at something north of 20,000 feet which I assumed meant that the rest of the trip would be relatively uneventful, except perhaps for the landing in New York. Wishful thinking on my part. Approximately 12-15 minutes into the flight, the pilot asked me through my headset if I would like to have something to tell my grandchildren.

"*No*, thank you," I quickly and emphatically replied.

He laughed and proceeded to launch us into a long spiral dive followed by a steep climb and finally a series of stomach churning barrel rolls. I did manage to hold onto my lunch but my brain felt totally scrambled and disoriented. The rest of the trip was much easier on my cardio-vascular and digestive systems and we landed safely at the Suffolk County Air Force Base in Westhampton Beach barely 45 minutes after take-off.

As we rolled to a stop, I thanked the pilot, climbed down from the cockpit, got on my hands and knees, and literally kissed the tarmac. I was that relieved to be back on Mother Earth. Although the pilot offered to get permission to pick me up at the end of my 72-hour pass, I politely thanked him but indicated that I would be fine flying back commercial, convinced that I had just outwitted the Grim Reaper and not wanting to tempt fate again so soon. Final note: the flight back to Charleston via National Airlines was incredibly slow, tedious, and frankly, rather boring.

The second experience, and in many ways the most relaxing, involved Captain Hasty's tiny H-13 Huey single passenger helicopter. I had already flown in the helicopter roughly a dozen times as part of my Casualty Notification and Survivors Assistance duties. Those trips, always to isolated locations within South Carolina, were inherently stressful thanks to the nature of the message I was delivering, although Captain Hasty certainly did everything in his power to relieve some of that pressure during the flights.

The fun part of my H-13 experience came towards the end of my Charleston assignment. I had arrived at the office at 0730 on a nice early spring morning and was reviewing my schedule for the day when I heard the distinctive **THWOP, THWOP, THWOP** sound of a helicopter overhead. Not a particularly unusual sound in a military city like Charleston, but the sound did seem a bit closer than normal. No sooner had I accepted the fact that perhaps it was just my imagination when, to my total surprise, the chopper landed on the parade ground just outside my office window. I immediately recognized it as Captain Hasty's although I couldn't imagine why he was there. I had no new Casualty Notification cases requiring air transportation nor did I have any ongoing Survivors Assistance cases in outlying areas. The answer came quickly from Captain Hasty as he bounded into my office.

"I have been instructed by Colonel Campbell to give you a complete aerial tour of Charleston and the Lowcountry. Bring your camera and let's get airborne." This was a treat that I knew I was going to thoroughly enjoy!

And so, we lifted off from the parade ground and spent the next couple of hours flying over the Depot, the city, and outlying areas, at altitudes ranging from 500 to 2000 feet depending upon the type of picture I wanted to take. Whenever I chose a target, he would bank the helicopter sharply to the right while dropping down to whatever altitude I requested. The benefit of the sharp right bank was immediately apparent: the H-13 had no doors, thereby allowing me to take perfectly clear and unobstructed pictures of my target. Once I adjusted to literally looking straight down from those altitudes while being held in place by just a simple seat belt/shoulder harness, I was able to take some great pictures for posterity. Yet another once in a lifetime experience.

A third unique flying experience, and certainly the most harrowing, came roughly midway through my assignment to Charleston. It involved a single engine vintage pre-World War II surplus Army Air Corp plane owned and operated by a truly grizzled war veteran by the

name of Arthur D. Poole. Captain Poole had come up
through the ranks; an enlisted man in the Army Air Corps
during World War II, an army pilot and warrant officer
during the Korean Conflict, and a three-time volunteer for
tours of duty in Vietnam as a helicopter pilot. His military
personnel "201" file listed numerous awards received
during his long career including, but by no means limited
to, several Bronze Stars for heroism, a few Purple Hearts
for wounds received in combat and so on. To say that he
was a big-time risk-taker would be massive understatement.
As a case in point, his most recent assignment prior to
Charleston says it all: a year in Vietnam dropped behind
enemy lines with his crew to repair and fly out downed
helicopters.

    With that as a backdrop, and although I had great
respect for the captain, I was not especially keen on the
thought of flying with him in his vintage plane. Well,
maybe a short flight on a beautiful day would be fun.
Unfortunately, it didn't work out that way. Early one
morning, Captain Poole asked me to join him on a routine
flight from Charleston to Fort Jackson in Columbia, a two-
hour car ride up I-26 and about a one-hour trip by air. I say
unfortunately because the weather was dreadful, heavy
rain, fog, high winds, with occasional thunderstorms in the
forecast. Nevertheless, he had an appointment scheduled at
Fort Jackson which he did not want to miss, so off we
drove to the Air Base. My naive assumption was that once
we arrived at the terminal, he would realize that a drive up
I-26 was the best way to meet his deadline. My fallback
hope was that the air traffic controllers would simply not
allow a takeoff under such dreadful conditions. Needless to
say, neither of those options panned out. The air traffic
controllers did their best to talk the captain out of the flight,
warning him of unpredictable weather on the trip, perhaps
even including a tornado watch in the vicinity. Wonderful!
Nothing was going to deter the good captain from making

this trip. Nor was he going to allow me to wimp out at the last minute.

Not surprisingly, we were the only plane taking off under those conditions. The plane was buffeted on both sides as it gathered speed down the runway and, with a final thrust, somehow became airborne. Visibility? Well, there was none as far as I could see, as we headed off in what I presumed was a northwesterly direction, pretty much paralleling I-26, just above the treetops. The flight was hair-raising in every respect: high winds tossing the plane in every direction, torrential rain, and an intermittent fog. In other words, an absolutely ideal challenge for Captain Poole.

To put it in perspective, picture the minister's maniacal laugh on the 18th green during a thunderstorm in the classic comedy, "Caddyshack". The grizzled Captain Poole was having the time of his life while I, on the other hand, was holding on for dear life having concluded that this was definitely the doomed flight I had always feared and expected. Well, in spite of the odds, we managed to land safely at Ft. Jackson and by the time his meeting was over two hours later, the weather had cleared and the trip back home was pleasantly calm for me, although clearly boring for Captain Poole.

Another unique opportunity came to me totally out of the blue on an early Saturday morning in the summer of 1966. As the Duty Officer of the day, I received a call at home from our guard post at the Depot seeking advice on how to handle a trespasser who, oddly enough, had been dropped off by a small boat at our marina and was fishing off our dock. They described him as a somewhat older man, by himself, and dressed in casual clothes. Should they hold him for trespassing, bring him to the guard post for questioning, or simply ask him to leave? Curious as to why anyone would pick that spot to fish with so many other choice spots readily available both up and down the river, I told them to do nothing until I got there. There certainly were no military secrets at the marina, filled as it was with vintage tug boats, other harbor craft, and World War II LCM's and LCU's. When I checked in at the guard post I told them to sit tight until I returned from the dock area.

Once there, I approached the fisherman who turned and introduced himself to me although that was totally unnecessary. Standing across from me in casual fishing gear, plaid shirt, black cotton pants, and a floppy hat with various fishing lures attached, was the highest ranking active duty military officer in the heavily populated military environment of Charleston, none other than Rear Admiral Thomas Dorsey. His responsibilities were well known to all in the military and were impressive: stationed at the vast Charleston Naval Base, he was the Commodore of the Navy's 6th Fleet, covering roughly one-half of the Atlantic Ocean from the Arctic to Antarctica. In hindsight, probably a very good thing that I had taken a casual approach to this "trespasser"! The natural question was why, with several miles of river frontage available to him at the Naval Base, was he fishing at the Army Depot? His answer was simple and logical and spoke to the man I was to come to know.

"Here I can relax and fish in peace and quiet and put all my cares away for a couple of hours. At the Naval Base peace and quiet is not an option available to me."

He then gave me an extra fishing pole and we sat there together in relative silence for an hour or so after which he headed off to an appointment.

The admiral continued to fish off the Depot dock, almost always very early on a Saturday morning, frequently calling ahead to the guard post to make sure that I was alerted just in case I wanted to sit with him and try my luck which I often did. As it turned out, our luck was not very good but that did not seem to bother him in the least. For him, it was all about R&R away from the firing line. He did, over time, also become somewhat more talkative, focusing primarily on his love of the City of Charleston and the surrounding Lowcountry, his hope to retire there, and my Grim Reaper duties at the Depot. Although we never specifically discussed the war in Vietnam, I certainly sensed that he was getting frustrated by the staggering loss of American lives as well as by the overall direction that our effort seemed to be taking.

The unique opportunity offered by the admiral came shortly before I completed my posting to the Army Depot: a full day's trip into the Atlantic Ocean submerged in a nuclear submarine. Once again my demons beckoned. Was it possible that I was claustrophobic? I had absolutely no idea; however, I was sure that a full day submerged in a tube, even a very large one, would certainly test that possibility. Yet there it was: another once in a lifetime opportunity that I simply couldn't pass up.

On the morning of my scheduled dive, I drove over to the Naval Submarine Base up on Goose Creek, was directed at the gate to my objective, and was welcomed aboard by the captain, an extremely gracious man who sensed my apprehension and assured me that a touch of nerves was very common before anyone's first underwater trip. According to him, even veterans of submarine combat remember their fears before their first dive. The key, he emphasized, was to focus on the job at hand, which in my case was to learn as much as possible about the day to day functions carried out by the crew. We left Charleston Harbor at approximately 0630 and by the time we reached the Atlantic, I was so involved with observing the crew at work, that I had no concerns whatsoever about what lay just ahead...the day underwater. Quite a contrast to all of my flying experiences.

As a follow-up to that observation, I should note that a number of years later while working on Wall Street, I recruited a new client in Washington D.C., a long time nuclear submarine captain who had participated in one memorable tour of duty during the Cold War – submerged under the polar cap ice for several months. Just thinking about that still gives me very real claustrophobic feelings. One day was a great experience: several months, a frightening thought.

On terra firma, I also enjoyed a more mundane and on-going challenge: the weekly Charleston Army Depot Bowling League which pitted one military team, both officers and non-coms against eight to ten teams of civilian employees. We met on Tuesday evenings and the competitive atmosphere was intense with all the civilian teams dedicated to knocking off the military team and the military team equally committed to victory. In hindsight, we probably started off with a significant advantage. Several members of our team, and Colonel Campbell in particular, were flat out good bowlers, very competitive and with years of league experience behind them. Amazingly, in spite of his busy schedule, the colonel never missed a single week over the three-year life of the league, frequently racing back from political dinners and the like in time to compete, often responding to my look of surprise with a shrug of his shoulders and an emphatic "I know my priorities" retort. Bottom line: we won most of our weekly matches and, on an overall basis, came out on top of the league standings in 1965, 1966, and 1967.

My personal high came towards the end of my third year. I had proven to be a decent bowler but certainly not in the top echelon of our league; however on that one night, I was "in the zone" with an opening game of 186, followed by an even better 196. My final game began with four quick strikes followed by additional strikes in the fifth and sixth frames, not all that unusual for a top bowler but rarified air for me. At that point in time, bowlers in nearby lanes started to notice my score on the overhead scoreboard and by the time I made strikes in the seventh and eighth frames, I knew that I had something special going on. So apparently did the manager of the place who took it upon himself to announce over the loud speaker that, "Lt. Motz is going for a perfect game in the ninth frame over on lane 23."

The reaction was instantaneous. We all know how loud a bowling alley can be, especially on league nights. Well, that roar evaporated in an instant leaving an eerie and deafening silence. I did manage to strike again in the ninth frame, and although I knew intuitively that my teammates were hurrying their games to make it easier for me, everything seemed to be moving in slow motion. My first ball in the tenth frame was yet another strike bringing me to the threshold of bowling immortality. It was not to be. My second ball was the dreaded 7-10 split leaving me with a final score of 289. No "300 Club" for me.

The ironic footnote to this story played out the following month as I headed home from Charleston. A stop on the way to visit my twin sister Susan and her husband, Dick, in Philadelphia mandated that I show them my high game trophy. Naturally, she challenged me to a match at a local bowling alley that night where she proceeded to beat me quite handily in all three games. So much for any risk of my ego getting out of control!

CHAPTER 15

Dating Southern Belles:
My uphill battle for acceptance.

As challenging as some of my part-time assignments were, and as enjoyable as my off-duty downtime was, my experiences dating the true "southern belle" were in a league of their own. Not easy to move forward in a new relationship burdened by several potentially disqualifying marks on your dating resume.

Long before that handful of distraught young widows had developed a short-term, purely psychological crush on me as they went through the horrors of dealing with the death of their husbands, my actual dating life in Charleston had been pretty abysmal. Certainly, my unpredictable work schedule was partly to blame. More significantly; however, I quickly learned that dating a Southern girl carried with it certain obstacles not encountered up North, either in New York or during my college days in Washington, D.C. Yes, some of those challenges centered around my Catholicism and/or my status in the military, as highlighted in my earlier comments on prejudice. Beyond those stumbling blocks; however, was one of far greater import: I was a Yankee, and a Yankee from New York City to boot. It quickly became very obvious to me that any new relationship was likely to fail simply because I was not a Charlestonian or, at the very least, from another acceptable enclave within the Deep South.

"We were taught from early childhood not to trust you fast talkin' men from up North." Hard to exaggerate how many times I heard variations of that comment, usually during a second or third date.

It was also made abundantly clear that if a Charleston girl was foolish enough to fall in love with me, I would be required to move permanently to Charleston since, "No self-respecting Charleston girl would ever consider living elsewhere, and certainly not in New York, not for you or, for that matter, for anyone else."

Not surprisingly, with that as a backdrop, my efforts to bridge that gap did lead to some rather challenging situations starting in April of 1965, my second month in Charleston. Early in that month, I received a call from Miss Margaret Riley, a "friend of a friend" of my mother, who offered to introduce me to some "proper young men and women" living in the city. Miss Riley, I learned, was a single woman in her late fifties, from a well-established local family, and the proprietor of a ladies dress shop in downtown Charleston. She invited me to her home on Tradd Street, a narrow one-way street in the heart of the exclusive "South of Broad Street" neighborhood at four o'clock on the following Saturday afternoon. I was happy to accept the invitation.

When I arrived at her home at the appointed hour, dressed in a blue and white striped button-down shirt, red tie, blue blazer, khaki pants, and black loafers, I was met at the door by Miss Riley who introduced me to a dozen or so men and women about my age, all of whom were very polite and "old school proper". They all seemed genuinely interested in my New York upbringing, speaking of it with alternating waves of awe and horror.

"Manhattan sounds like an amazing place but how in the world could anyone live there?" was the underlying theme voiced by all.

For some, I sensed that I may well have been a rare contact with a Yankee close to their age, save perhaps for a cadet or two enrolled at the Citadel. After brief conversations with many of them, I turned my focus to one particular girl who seemed the most intrigued by my background and, as I prepared to leave, asked her out for dinner the following Saturday evening. Surprisingly, she accepted and the date was set. I would pick her up at 7 o'clock and take her to the restaurant of her choice.

On the evening of the date, I drove to the address she had given me, parked my car, and gazed up at one of the grander homes in a neighborhood of nothing but grand homes. As I climbed the wide expanse of steps toward the front entrance, I marveled at the beautiful portico – several large white columns gracefully flanking a massive mahogany door. This was going to be an enjoyable evening even if my date and I failed to hit it off. My rather timid knock on the door brought no response so I tried again with a bit heavier hand. Still no response. Had she gotten cold feet and decided that she wanted no part of an evening with me? Certainly a possibility. After one final and futile pounding on the door, I retreated back down the steps and, as I was about to get into my car, tail between my legs, noticed a car parked behind the house. Perhaps the family was back there and hadn't heard my knock.

As I approached the back door, I saw movement inside in what appeared to be the kitchen and sure enough, my knock brought an immediate response from my date who opened the door with a big smile on her face. Suddenly, things were beginning to look more promising. Her parents also greeted me enthusiastically, welcoming me into their home. Quite naturally, the first words out of my mouth after introductions were made focused on my praise of their beautiful home, mentioning in passing that I would truly enjoy getting a personal tour. For reasons I did not understand at that time, that request was left hanging and the topic changed by the parents to my life in the Army, my assignment to Charleston, my impressions of their city, and so on.

For dinner, she chose the Colony House, one of the finer downtown restaurants in those days, and I soon learned, her favorite place for a nice, quiet dinner. The prime rib that it was known for was excellent, the atmosphere just right, and as a result, conversation flowed easily, giving me a very positive "getting to know you" feeling.

As we spooned our dessert, a perfect chocolate mousse, curiosity got the better of me and I asked her why her parents had chosen not to pick up on my wish for a tour of their home. I specifically wanted to make sure that I hadn't offended them with my request.

Her answer threw me completely off-guard. "We don't live in that part of the house. My sister, my parents, and I live in a sectioned-off four rooms in the rear of the house. "Why?" you ask. Because it just costs too much to maintain the whole place, electricity, heat, repairs, whatever."

This led to what I thought at that time was a logical follow-up question. "Why then don't your parents consider selling their home and buying another more manageable one somewhere else in the neighborhood?"

To say that comment put an end to our budding relationship would be well beyond understatement. She looked at me as if I had just suggested that perhaps her parents should consider selling off their daughters into slavery to cover their expenses.

"Our home has been in our family for well over one hundred years, since before the Civil War, and we will never sell it under any circumstances. *Never!* You Yankees just don't understand or have any respect or appreciation for tradition. Please be kind enough to *take me home, immediately!*"

Those last words spoken very loudly for all to hear as she pushed herself up from the table. End of date and budding relationship.

With that rejection during my second month in Charleston, I foolishly assumed that my luck on the dating circuit could only get better. It did not. Nothing quite as dramatic as that initial experience for sure, but discouraging nevertheless. Typically, the young ladies in the Charleston area seemed to enjoy a first date with me but by the second or third date, they invariably became wary of me and progressively more and more distant.

In an effort to stem that tide and improve my luck, one of my fellow officers at the Depot thought that a double date with him might help to break that pattern. Dave, also a single lieutenant who had grown up in Biloxi, Mississippi, was a true conservative southerner in every respect. Heck, at the age of 25 he was still attending Sunday School classes at the local Methodist Church, joining mostly high school and college-age students. Yet, in spite of our very different backgrounds, we did enjoy golfing together on occasion, and testing our angling skills on the Unit Fund deep sea fishing trips.

Dave had been dating a girl from Savannah, Georgia for several months, travelling there many weekends to spend time with her. Although it sounded like a rather desperate measure to take, I agreed to accompany him, mainly to get my first look at the city itself which was considered to be the antebellum "kissing cousin" of Charleston. Dave's girlfriend assured me that she had a perfect match in mind for me, a nice girl she had known all her life whom she thought would enjoy meeting a guy from New York.

My first impression of my date was very positive. She was very attractive, charming, and definitely from the upper-tier of Savannah society. She seemed genuinely fascinated to hear about life up North although it soon became very clear to me that it was a part of the country she had little interest in visiting much less moving to on a permanent basis. That aside, even if she had been able to negotiate that "Yankee hurdle", I simply could not negotiate my hurdle with her: her idea of humor. Granted, she was a very gifted joke-teller, one of the best I had ever heard, surprisingly bawdy, with a flawless Southern drawl, and spot-on delivery of the punch lines. Sadly; however, every single joke she told, and she had a seemingly endless supply of them, were blatantly racist. Honestly, I don't think she missed a single negative stereotype about "the coloreds"– her choice of words because as she eloquently stated, "I know you Yankees prefer to call the niggers the coloreds," although that substitution was not used in any of her jokes because, she maintained, "it would destroy the essence and flow of the joke." Yet another one date and out.

I finally hit my dating stride in the late autumn of 1965, thanks indirectly and unintentionally to Dave. We had been called over to the Depot one Saturday morning to complete a project prior to an upcoming inspection and for convenience sake, we took the short trip together in his car. Interestingly enough, it was my only local trip as a passenger in his car and it led to a seminal event in my life. As we drove back from the Depot several hours later, we passed the Methodist Church where he worshipped and he noticed a young woman sitting on the lawn in front of a home directly across from the church.

"Hey, that's Brenda. She's in my Sunday School class. Let's stop and say hey."

Why not, I thought. Brenda was a very attractive blond of college age and she greeted Dave warmly as he introduced her to me. We spoke for several minutes and then took off for home. As we pulled away from her home, I turned around to take a final look at her and she winked at me. One simple wink. When I told Dave that I might ask her out he laughed and told me in no uncertain terms that I would be wasting my time.

"She won't go out with me and she certainly won't go out with a Yankee. Believe me, I tried to talk her into a date for over a year and never got anywhere with her."

Well, I knew her first and last name and I knew where she lived, so I called her up as soon as I got home and asked her if she would like to spend the afternoon on the beach at Isle of Palms.

"I'd love to," she replied.

That singular stroke of good luck, karma, destiny, or whatever you would want to call it, led to a short relationship with Brenda who then traded me in for a Southern boy, followed by a romance with her older sister, Mary, our marriage in late 1967, and our four children.

CHAPTER 16

Orders to Vietnam:
An assignment that seemed inevitable.

Whether I was working with families devastated by the loss of their loved one, off on one of my other assignments, or just having a good time, the high probability of an assignment to Vietnam was never far from my mind. Not that I found that possibility frightening or even undesirable, just unsettling. I was not alone. Every Army officer on active duty from the mid-1960s thru the early 1970s knew that the odds favored an eventual assignment to Vietnam. I was certainly no exception. Far from it. On three separate occasions, spread out between mid-1965 and mid-1969, I found myself facing that very real possibility.

My first brush with Vietnam came less than six months into my Charleston posting and it was, in a sense, a fluke. The Army, in an effort to fully exploit its superior helicopter capability on a battlefield ideally suited for rotary-wing aircraft had, under orders from President Lyndon Johnson, created a new division, christened the First Cavalry Division (Airmobile). The support ship for that mission, eventually renamed the Corpus Christi Bay, was scheduled to be reconfigured at the Charleston Naval Shipyard under the guidance of an Army warrant officer temporarily assigned to our Depot.

In the months prior to the arrival of that ship, I had spent a good deal of time talking to him and became increasingly intrigued by the idea of volunteering to join that new unit. Why would I even think about doing such a thing? Well, overall troop deployment to Vietnam had accelerated quite dramatically during the spring and early summer of '65, making it more likely than ever that I would soon be there, so why not volunteer to join the First

Airmobile and put that seemingly inevitable assignment behind me. After all, it was an elite state-of-the-art unit, and the ship was scheduled to be anchored just off the coast of Cam Rahn Bay in the South China Sea.

The temptation to volunteer for that assignment increased even further with the surprise arrival on August 16 of two huge troop transports, the USNS Darby, T-AP-127, and the USNS Buckner, T-AP-123. Two old ships dating back to World War II, now in our marina preparing to load troops of the Second Brigade plus various support commands for the month-long voyage to the East Coast of Vietnam.

Colonel Campbell understood my logic and had no problem whatsoever in placing a call to the Pentagon on my behalf. Their response: the entire division had been in frenetic training for several months and would be entering the final prep stages aboard ship during the month-long cruise to the Far East. In other words, it was too late to add anyone to the unit. In hindsight, it was probably just as well. My Survivors Assistance work with retired Army personnel and active duty soldiers killed in action was keeping me very busy and the colonel suspected that he would soon be adding the first half of that program – Casualty Notification – to my resume.

My second brush with an assignment to Vietnam followed a more typical path, just as I was about to complete my first year of active duty. On a surprisingly chilly morning in early November of 1965 – November the third to be precise – Colonel Campbell called me into his office and, with a particularly solemn look on his face and in a somber voice, told me that he had just received orders from the Pentagon addressed to my attention concerning a new assignment. He then handed me the official release which spelled out the details. In two or three brief sentences, I was directed to report to the 96th Quartermaster Battalion in Ft. Riley, Kansas not later than

February the fifteenth, "for subsequent deployment to a restricted area overseas," a clear sign that I was on my way to Vietnam.

Since I was roughly halfway through my two-year active duty commitment, it would be disingenuous to suggest that the news came as a total surprise to me. Most young officers during that period in our history, who had served a year stateside under a two-year active duty commitment were being shipped overseas at the start of their second year, with the vast majority of them posted to a unit in Vietnam.

Naturally, word spread quickly around the Depot and the reaction was not unexpected. To a man, the other more senior officers, all career men, including two captains, two majors, and a lieutenant colonel genuinely viewed it as great news for me, a wonderful opportunity to enhance my military record on the battlefield thereby opening the possibility of quicker promotions down the road. Their assumption, of course, was that I was destined to be a "career man," far from a foregone conclusion in my mind at that time.

Colonel Campbell, on the other hand, had immediately and properly directed his focus toward the needs of the Depot and more specifically, on finding a replacement officer to take over my duties, in particular my work with families dealing with the death of a loved one. Unknown to me at the time, he was also sizing up my reaction to the news, quite possibly suspecting that I was not fully committed to a career in the military and therefore just might be willing to remain in Charleston to continue my work with those families. Not surprisingly, the civilian employees took the news in stride. They all understood that reassignments were a fact of life in the military. They were the permanent employees of the Depot; we were merely the transients.

In all honesty, the news did catch me more off-guard than I would have thought. On the one hand, having witnessed the tragic result of war on an almost daily basis, I certainly understood the risks of a direct battlefield posting. On the other hand, since I had not completely ruled out a career in the Army, I clearly recognized that a year served in Vietnam could indeed become a significant positive should I choose to remain on active duty.

I naturally wondered what my new assignment might be, a question that the colonel was able to answer with a follow-up call to the Pentagon that afternoon. I would be assigned to a Quartermaster slot, the MOS (Military Occupational Specialty) for which I had trained during my posting to Ft. Lee. In addition, they indicated that, because of my Survivors Assistance work at the Depot, I most likely would be put in charge of a Graves Registration unit with the responsibility of retrieving, identifying, and body-bagging soldiers killed in action on the battlefield and then preparing them for shipment to the embalming facility at Tachikawa Air Force Base in Japan.

One thing was certain: I had to assume that I would be leaving Charleston sometime within that three-plus month period. Fortunately, the lease on my apartment was on a month-to-month basis and I really had very little personal property of any significant value. Yes, there was my new color television set and some furniture that would need to be stored somewhere, but that was about it, except for one major item: my brand new 1966 Corvette convertible. I just loved that car.

To digress for a moment, I had bought the car on a lark just a few weeks earlier, having seen it prominently displayed in the showroom window of the local Chevrolet dealership as I drove downtown on East Bay. It was love at first sight. Of course, I realized that it was undoubtedly way out of my price range; nevertheless, I found myself drawn into the showroom to take a closer look. Up close, it was even more gorgeous than I had imagined, a white convertible with a bright red upholstered interior. The shock came when I looked at the price tag, $3,750, about half of what I had expected. Without hesitation, I blurted out, "I'll take it" to the salesman standing nearby. One of my better impulse purchases. That price, by the way, worked out to just about one half of my annual military salary at that time. Thank God for a modest but very welcome inheritance from my Aunt Sue and Uncle Charlie.

The car proved to be a ton of fun with only one negative: me driving it in the Deep South with my New York State vanity license plate, GM-2. Talk about a magnet for all types of law enforcement personnel, local and state alike, who were delighted to pull over a Yankee driving a fancy new sports car with a personalized license plate. The saving grace: my Army identification card. Yes, I was pulled over on occasion; however, not a single ticket was issued to me during the entire time I drove it throughout the military friendly South.

Breaking the news of my new assignment to my family, especially to my mother, presented a most important challenge, something I felt I needed to do in person. Yes, I realized that she fully understood that I might end up in Vietnam. After all, she had been the one to encourage me to join the R.O.T.C. program at Georgetown with that very possibility in mind. Of course, I also knew that she was praying that it would not happen. One thing for sure, it certainly would cause her to focus on our family history which included a couple of close relatives who had lost their lives fighting for our country: my uncle, Archie Motz toward the end of World War I, and then my first cousin and godfather, Mickey Motz, killed in action on January the eighth of 1945 during one of the key battles of World War II, the month-long Battle of the Bulge, for which he was awarded the Silver Star for gallantry.

The most logical next step was to grab a 72-hour pass, fly back to New York to alert my family, and then return to Charleston. Fortunately, I had no funerals scheduled during that period, so I met with the two families with funerals scheduled for the following week, promising them that I would visit them just as soon as I returned from New York. That accomplished, I was on my way to the airport by 0600 the following morning.

Needless to say, my unannounced arrival back home that evening was a genuine surprise to my mother, a happy surprise, at first. When I told her the reason for my visit; however, her mood quickly turned considerably less festive. Naturally, she was very concerned for my safety, but she was also an incredibly strong woman in her own quiet way. I explained to her that the assignment was still a bit up in the air because of my ongoing Survivors Assistance work, but that I fully expected to be shipped out once my replacement was assigned to the Depot. In any event, she pitched in to help me put things in order allowing me to head back to Charleston on a non-stop flight from Kennedy Airport the following evening.

Back in Charleston, I turned my full attention to the two open active duty Survivors Assistance cases, visiting with both families, reassuring them that I would be there for the memorial service. Not surprisingly, on my first day back at the office, I received a call from the Presidio requesting that I begin Survivors Assistance for a local family whose son had been killed in Vietnam. This, of course, only served to highlight a glaring void at the Depot. Yes, I would be able to help that family but at some point, I would be gone, with no replacement yet assigned to our facility. Moreover, it was abundantly clear to the colonel that none of the other officers stationed at the Depot wanted any part of my assignment, even on a temporary basis. Add to that dilemma, the new Casualty Notification program was about to be officially launched and I was the one trained for that delicate assignment.

This very obvious problem, I would discover much

later, had prompted Colonel Campbell to place yet another call to the Pentagon in which he flat out stated, "I can't let Lt. Motz go until you ship his replacement to us. No ifs, ands, or buts."

Totally by coincidence, the colonel had been at a political dinner the night before that call and had engaged Congressman L. Mendel Rivers in a lengthy conversation which briefly touched on that issue. I had met the congressman on several occasions during various ceremonies at the Depot and he always seemed very appreciative of my efforts on behalf of his constituents.

Obviously, the congressman had considerable clout: the following day my orders to Ft. Riley were put on temporary hold while the Pentagon and the congressman sorted things out. The final decision came from the Pentagon on February the seventh, one week prior to my scheduled reporting date: I was more valuable to the Army remaining in Charleston continuing my work with bereaved families, especially, they noted, with the new Casualty Notification regulations scheduled to be implemented the following month.

My third and final potential assignment to Vietnam came slightly more than three years later, in early June of 1969. At that time, I was on reserve duty assigned to a Transportation unit based at Ft. Totten, an Army post in New York City. As a reservist, I was obligated to spend two weekends a month at Ft. Totten in addition to annual summer camps at Camp Drum in upstate New York.

By that time, I was also well into my third year as a security analyst on Wall Street. The surprising news came via the "broad-tape," the euphemism for the printed newswire that accompanied the ticker-tape of stock quotations. The broad-tape existed to keep Wall Streeters up-to-date on late breaking news; corporate or macro-economic news as well as world news of interest to investors. Our firm had a broad-tape reader, Harvey

Palmer, assigned to shout out news items during the course of the day. In early June, as I was sitting at my desk reviewing a report I had written on the tire & rubber industry, I heard Harvey call out, "A transportation unit out of Ft. Totten has been called to active duty, effective immediately." That certainly got my attention! A call to my unit confirmed that my battalion had indeed received a stand-by alert and that the details of the order would be forthcoming within 24 hours.

Since I was literally weeks away from completing my six-year commitment, married with one child and a second one on the way, and very much into my evolving Wall Street career, I was somewhat less than thrilled at the thought of getting back into my fatigues and going off to war. Nevertheless, I knew that if it came to pass, I would, of course, just make the necessary adjustments. In this case, the Hand of Providence was watching over me. The follow-up order from the Pentagon the next day indicated that all units of my battalion would be heading off to Vietnam *except,* for some unfathomable reason, my platoon. Two weeks later, on June the twelfth, I received my Honorable Discharge.

Over the years, I have often asked myself if I would have benefitted from an assignment to Vietnam. Certainly, as a life experience, I would have to say yes; however, my service stateside to distraught families in their time of need was, without a doubt, the single most important factor in establishing the guideposts by which I have strived to lead my life.

EPILOGUE

The Military Experience in Perspective:
It was a memorable ride.

My assignment to Charleston was a true blessing in so many ways. I quickly fell in love with the city and surrounding Lowcountry for its pure beauty and southern charm, and with the people, black and white alike, with whom I developed a number of special relationships. Yes, it was a bit strange arriving there as I did in the late winter of 1964-'65 to find many of the locals preparing to celebrate the centennial of their victory in the "War Against Northern Aggression".

"We did not lose the war. We are still here one hundred years later and our way of life is basically as it was before the war. Last time I checked, the North was not occupying our land. Quite the contrary: you Yankees can't seem to get enough of us, spending all your vacations with us and, in many cases, retiring among us to enjoy all that we have to offer: our climate, culture, food, and laidback lifestyle."

Hard to argue against that logic which was embraced by a surprisingly large number of South Carolinians, and not just those who might be classified as rednecks. That aside, just about everyone I met while living in Charleston, though very proud of their heritage, were very friendly to me, in spite of my "Yankee" roots. Well, except when it came to romance with a southern belle. There the bar was set considerably higher.

One thing for sure: those two-and-one-half years of active duty proved to be a very important building block for my subsequent careers in the non-military world. The military's philosophy of entrusting important responsibilities to young officers was immeasurably helpful to me as I turned my focus to a Wall Street career at the still relatively tender age of 25. Clearly, the Casualty Notification and Survivors Assistance assignments, while difficult from an emotional perspective, did give me a solid sense of accomplishment, while at the same time probably giving me a maturity beyond my years.

Of far greater importance, those responsibilities also offered me a rare opportunity to meet and come to understand a segment of society totally foreign to me fifty years ago – the Southern black family. To a man, woman, and child, I found them all to be warm, caring people, able to deal with the devastating news I was obligated to give them through a combination of a remarkably stoic outlook on life, almost always combined with a strong religious foundation.

The military life itself also gave me the opportunity to meet and work directly with a number of extremely successful people, either within the armed forces or in related federal or state government agencies. I learned a great deal from all of them simply by observing how they handled stressful situations, always with a high level of self-confidence and virtually always with positive results. That experience proved to be a tremendous help to me throughout my forty-two-year Wall Street career as well as during my four terms as the mayor of my special little village on the East End of Long Island. Totally different career paths, yet both aided considerably by valuable leadership lessons learned while on active duty.

Lieutenant General Louis W. Truman of the Third U.S. Army, for whom I worked on that challenging "transfer of affections" case, taught me how to face head-on, objectively analyze, and resolve troublesome issues quickly and decisively and, once resolved, to properly reward those who contributed to that successful resolution. That hair-raising flight home to the Hamptons aboard the Phantom fighter jet was truly memorable as was the surprise 72-hour furlough to visit family and friends.

Rear Admiral Thomas Dorsey, Commander of the 6th Fleet with whom I spent several Saturday mornings casually fishing at the Depot dock, taught me the importance of pacing myself, of learning how to take a guilt-free break now and then and how best to use that downtime for maximum benefit. Frankly, the mere fact that he took those two or three hours some Saturday mornings to recharge his batteries, taught me a valuable lesson: work hard with total focus on your work and then play hard with equal focus and energy.

General Mark Clark, a major force on the African Front during World War II, commander of United Nations ground forces during the Korean War, and then long-time president of the Citadel, actively encouraged me to pass on my practical military experience to his young cadets. The mere fact that he asked me to address his cadets in a formal classroom environment, spoke volumes about his understanding of the importance of keeping training in touch with the times. My singular message to those cadets was based on my own personal experience: as young Army officers, you will be expected to enthusiastically accept and master whatever assignment you are given, even if it bears little or no resemblance to the specific work for which you were trained.

The politicians with whom I crossed paths also provided a rich and colorful experience for me. The irascible Congressman L. Mendel Rivers, Chairman of the all-powerful House Armed Services Committee, who singlehandedly pulled me back from a Vietnam assignment to continue my work with his constituents, wielded his enormous influence to benefit the Charleston community. The major presence of all five branches of the service as well as a seemingly endless number of major defense contractors in his district spoke to his powerful clout and certainly were critically important factors supporting the local economy for many decades. Of equal importance was his sensitivity to local men and women serving in the military. Yes, he was an ardent segregationist for much of his life but he was able to remove color from his mind when it came to military sacrifice. To his everlasting credit, I cannot recall a single award ceremony at the Depot honoring a fallen soldier, black or white, where he was not a very visible presence, always taking time to individually thank those families for the sacrifice made by their loved one for their country.

Not to be forgotten, of course, was my priceless encounter at the Sunset Lodge with that "shall remain nameless" state official. From that individual I learned that things were often not as they appeared, especially in the world of politics.

The military life also gave me a once in a lifetime opportunity to travel from point "A" to point "B" in various modes of transportation. The shortest trip by far was aboard the huge LARC V amphibious vehicle which was designed as a replacement for World War II LCMs and LCUs. That trip one sunny afternoon, took me from the Depot harbor to the main gate, a trip of less than one mile, ending at its permanent place of honor as a lawn ornament at the entrance to the Depot, adjacent to a small pond, home to Charley, an aging alligator and Post mascot.

Not to be forgotten was the little H-13 Huey single passenger helicopter. Without it, my ability to reach out to families living in isolated areas, especially the Gullah/Geechee people, would have been severely compromised. In addition, the "fun" trip orchestrated by Colonel Campbell and Captain Hasty toward the end of my tour of duty was flat out special. The pictures that I took of Charleston, the Depot, and the beautiful outlying plantations throughout the Lowcountry are irreplaceable and the source of many fond memories.

The two special plane trips I took were the polar opposites of each other, yet both thrilling in their own unique way. The fighter jet trip was both nerve-wracking and exciting and it certainly did give me something to tell my grandchildren. The other, aboard the pre-World War II vintage single engine plane piloted by Captain Poole, was just plain nerve-wracking in the extreme. Was I impressed with Captain Poole's ability to safely navigate his plane under those horrid weather conditions? Of course I was; nevertheless, I did not volunteer for any follow-up trips, suspicious that the Grim Reaper was awaiting that moment to finally surface in my life.

Yet another special and memorable treat was that full day submerged aboard the nuclear submarine, compliments of Admiral Dorsey. It was an amazing experience right up there with the fighter flight and if it proved anything, I guess it did show me that I wasn't quite as claustrophobic as I feared, probably not a bad thing to know about myself.

As important as all of those experiences were to me, none were more gratifying than two very special events arranged for me, the first of which took place in the latter half of 1966, the second during my last full month of active duty in the early spring of 1967. Both took me completely by surprise and have remained among the most positive memories of my entire life.

The first one began with a call from one of the black ministers with whom I had worked on a number of funerals in the outlying areas of Charleston. He asked if he could pick me up at the Depot the following morning and take me to meet some of his friends. For reasons I could not have known at the time, he gave me no more information about the trip nor did I ask for any. He picked me up in the morning and told me that we were going to St. Helena Island in Beaufort County, about an hour-and-a-half south of Charleston. Still no clue as to the purpose of the trip. When we arrived on the island, he drove us to a little community with the unusual name of Frogmore, where we were greeted by several men outside a building named the Penn Center. That name rang a bell with me. I remembered it from my college history lessons as an early center for civil rights activities in South Carolina.

Following introductions, I was invited into the center by the minister, telling me as we walked, that he had someone he wanted me to meet. That person was Dr. Martin Luther King, Jr., who was there for a Southern Christian Leadership Conference meeting scheduled for later in the day. Dr. King had been asked by a number of the black ministers with whom I had been working to thank me for showing sensitivity to the black community during their difficult times. Now the secrecy made perfect sense. It was well-known at that time that certain elements would have welcomed the opportunity to disrupt the meeting or harm Dr. King if given the opportunity. We shook hands and he simply said, "I have heard wonderful things about your work with my people in their time of great need and I appreciate it. Thank you for caring." The meeting lasted only a minute or two, but the memory of it has lasted a lifetime.

The second memorable event took place in March of 1967 and it was a perfect ending to my Charleston experience. The leaders of the black community came together, led by black ministers, black funeral home directors, black politicians, and a number of other distinguished black citizens of the Greater Charleston area to throw a farewell dinner in my honor. The meal itself was wonderful and the comments made to me during the course of that evening were far more generous than I deserved but very much appreciated. As I thanked them for their kind words, I made the point that they were the true heroes for the manner in which they worked tirelessly with bereaved families in their time of need. All in all, a very special evening for me.

Finally, and above all, the driving force behind all

of my military experiences was my commanding officer, Colonel C.S. Campbell. Colonel Campbell commanded great respect at the Depot and throughout the military and civilian community in the greater Charleston area. His decisions were carefully considered and always fair and objective. Tough when he had to be, he also was comfortable displaying a sensitive side when appropriate.

That sensitivity was first evident to me in the late autumn of 1965. I was admitted to the Charleston Naval Hospital with severe abdominal pain, examined over a two-day period, and released with a final diagnosis of severe food poisoning. My appendix ruptured later that night and I was readmitted very early the next morning – Thanksgiving Day. Fortunately, the admitting doctor, Dr. James Martin, who coincidently lived in Army housing at the Depot, correctly diagnosed my illness and performed a six-hour surgery, very likely saving my life.

I remained hospitalized for close to a month following the surgery and during that time, Colonel Campbell visited me every single day, always bringing me newspapers, magazines and, most importantly, all the latest gossip from the Depot.

Bottom line: Colonel Campbell was a dedicated career officer who taught me invaluable lessons about life, leadership, and how to nail the pesky 7-10 split at the bowling alley.

A FIFTY-YEAR RETROSPECTIVE

Can it really be fifty years?

Without question, my two-and-one-half-years of active duty gave me a new perspective on life. Yes, the steady diet of casualty notifications and memorial services forced me to mature quickly. No question about that. Yet, of more lasting significance, the experience opened my eyes to a slice of life unfamiliar to me during my formative years; the world of war, poverty, and prejudice. I simply cannot imagine a more powerful wake-up call.

Over the years I have been asked if living within the shadow of death virtually every day left me with a permanent emotional scar, and I can honestly say that it did not. How is that possible? The answer is quite simple: the undeniable stress associated with each in-person death notification was largely offset by the positive steps that I was able to offer those families thanks to the Army's follow-up Survivors Assistance program. Without exception, every family I worked with during those tragic weeks following the death of their loved one genuinely appreciated the support they received and that, in turn, went a long way toward easing my stress level.

Needless to say, relieving my stress level was not the end game. The focus was always on the family: the devastating, life-changing impact of war on innocent families. Those soldiers were not senior citizens who had lived a long and successful life. Far from it. They were young men, indeed very young men, ranging in age from 18 to 29. Men with virtually their entire adult lives ahead of them, cut down in their prime in service to their country. An irreplaceable loss for all who loved them.

As I reflect back to those days, I have come to realize that my assignment also had a major impact on me, both as a parent and as an occasional mentor to other kids in need of emotional support and guidance. For example, if you asked any of my adult children what my foremost message was to them during their formative years, they would say, "Judge everyone not by the color of their skin but 'by the content of their character'," as so eloquently stated by Dr. Martin Luther King, Jr. in his iconic "I Have a Dream" speech at the Lincoln Memorial. One of my early mentors in life always liked to remind me that "Good people come in all shapes, sizes, colors, and religious beliefs. Find those good people and develop lifelong relationships with them. It's that simple." Would I have embraced that philosophy so fully had I not spent so much time working with those special families during that early period of my life? Possible, but I doubt it.

The idea of mentoring young inner-city kids came about quite by chance. Midway through my long Wall Street career, I developed solid business relationships with a number of prominent black professional athletes--highly skilled men, each with a laser-like focus on their career. Men who had made their mark and might be willing to give something back to their community. Clearly, they were in a unique position to be a positive influence on young men and women during their critically important teenage years, the time when lifelong habits, good or bad, are formed. Why not, I reasoned, introduce a few of those role-model athletes to vulnerable inner-city students in a formal student assembly with a follow-up, step-by-step mentoring program?

The initial reaction to this idea by most of the athletes was not surprising, "Hey, we're in the Big Apple for a couple of days every year and we want to have some fun."

Certainly understandable. To their credit, however, the reaction of every athlete as they finished their initial presentation to a rapt inner-city audience was striking. "When's the next one?" Remarkable! Once again, had I not had the experience of working with those distressed black families in their time of need, would I ever have thought of creating that program? I doubt it!

One thing for sure: I thoroughly embraced the challenges of the military life and remain impressed to this day by the life lessons learned. I was also very much taken by the professional manner in which the men and women with whom I served handled themselves and their assignments, as well as the camaraderie within the military community itself, a professional bonding unmatched by any of my life experiences before or since.

Working on this project has been a very rewarding experience for me, giving me the opportunity to once again relive those long-ago moments and frankly to gain a better understanding of just how important those few years were to me, something I had not thought much about as I put total focus on my growing family and my Wall Street career.

The only sadness comes from the stark realization that virtually all of the men and women who are the heart and soul of these stories have passed away, Colonel Campbell prematurely in his sixties many years ago and Doris Bercaw, in her eighties more recently. Quite naturally, that in turn, has also heightened an awareness of my own mortality.

One final thought which I briefly mentioned in the preface, and without a doubt the motivating factor that finally pushed me to finish this story: the horrible and senseless murders of nine members of the venerable Emanuel AME Church in downtown Charleston on June the 17th of 2015. Although it is often posited that something good comes from even the most horrific tragedies, one often has to dig very deep to prove that axiom. In this case, the proof comes from the powerful and very visible outpouring of love and compassion by the white population of Charleston, both immediately following the slaughter and to this day: a compassion I witnessed 50 years ago in my work, now visible for all to see.

In truth, my sadness will never completely dissipate since one of those victims was 87-year-old Miss Susie Jackson. Mother Emanuel was the site of several of my memorial services and Miss Susie was an integral part of those services, a truly wonderful and sensitive woman who worked tirelessly with the families of her church, who had suffered the unthinkable loss of a son during the Vietnam War. She, more than anyone else, helped me to understand the unique touches surrounding a funeral for a deceased black soldier, including the role of the "Professional Mourner." May she rest in peace.

ACKNOWLEDGEMENTS:

Who takes pen to paper, or in today's world, fingers to keyboard, to draft their first manuscript in their so-called 'golden years'? Probably not many, so please bear with me as I thank those who gave me my early love of writing, as well as those who, in more recent times, encouraged me to pursue this particular dream.

It all started with a lucky break during my high school years in Garden City, New York when I was assigned to a homeroom class presided over by the legendary John E. Warriner, creator of the widely read textbook – *Warriner's English Grammar and Composition*. Even better, I was also assigned to three of his English classes during those formative years.

Following graduation from Georgetown University and two plus years of active duty in the Army, I trained as a security analyst on Wall Street under the strict tutelage of Charlie Mott, who successfully stripped me of my college-based term paper tendency toward excessive verbiage.

More recently, as I contemplated finally taking the writing plunge, I bravely asked a friend, Sir Harold Evans, to read an early draft I had prepared. He agreed and responded with a justifiably harsh critique noting at the end; however, that I had a rare gift of narrative. "Go for it" he commanded! High praise from someone knighted by Queen Elizabeth for his excellence in investigative journalism.

Once committed to the project, I was ably supported and encouraged first by my cousin, Sue Palmieri and her husband Joe, and then by George Landegger, a Northerner by birth, transported to the Deep South during his adult life, the perfect person to add a unique fifty-year perspective on

TAPS

racial relations in both areas of our country.

Yet another invaluable perspective, a military one, was provided by a childhood friend, Tommy Richards, who grew up to become Rear Admiral Thomas R. Richards, Commander of a Naval Special Warfare Group, including the legendary Navy SEALS.

Thinking then that I had all bases covered, I gave a semifinal draft to my son Tim, a very talented and award-winning writer, who immediately drilled in on the central focus of my story. Thank you, Tim, for assuring that my focus remained on the true story – the horrible cost of war on families suffering the loss of a loved one.

Finally, my sincerest thanks to Jeanne McCarthy, a longtime friend and co-worker, who has provided strong technical support far beyond my limited capability, as well as unwavering patience through re-write after re-write.

Bottom line: thank you all for giving me the encouragement, support, and guidance during all stages of this process. I only hope I have done you justice.

INDEX

ABOUT THE AUTHOR:

George M. Motz earned a Bachelor's degree in history and philosophy as well as a commission as an officer in the United States Army from Georgetown University in June of 1963. Following graduation, he spent one year as a student at Fordham University School of Law and then opted to begin his two-year active duty commitment, initially at Ft. Lee in Petersburg, Virginia, and then at the Charleston Army Depot in Charleston, South Carolina. There he distinguished himself In the difficult fields of Casualty Notification & Survivors Assistance, for which he was awarded the Army Commendation Medal in 1967. Following his military service, he began a 40-year career on Wall Street, first as a security analyst, then as an asset manager, and eventually, as President and CEO of a boutique firm specializing in high net worth individuals. More recently, he served the Village of Quogue, New York, his adopted home, first on the Planning Board for many years and then through four terms as mayor. "Taps," a tribute to all families suffering the loss of a loved one in service to our country, is his first literary effort.

Made in the
USA
Middletown, DE